KAREN BEATTIE

2018

A BOOK OF GRACE-FILLED DAYS

LOYOLA PRESS.
A JESUIT MINISTRY

Chicago

LOYOLA PRESS.
A JESUIT MINISTRY

3441 N. Ashland Avenue
Chicago, Illinois 60657
(800) 621-1008
www.loyolapress.com

Cover and interior design by Kathy Kikkert.

ISBN-13: 978-0-8294-4464-3
ISBN-10: 0-8294-4464-5
Library of Congress Control Number: 2017942079

Printed in the United States of America.
17 18 19 20 21 22 23 24 Bang 10 9 8 7 6 5 4 3 2 1

About the Author

Karen Beattie is the author of *Rock-Bottom Blessings: Discovering God's Abundance When All Seems Lost*, which won an Excellence in Publishing Award from the Association of Catholic Publishers. She holds a master's degree in journalism and has written for several online and print publications including *America Magazine*, *Christianity Today*, and Patheos, among others. She also writes content for various businesses and creative agencies. Beattie has taught writing workshops and served as a judge for the ECPA Christian Book Awards®. She writes in the attic of her 1932 bungalow, where she lives with her husband and seven-year-old daughter on the West Side of Chicago.

Sing to the LORD a new song,
sing to the LORD, all you lands.
—PSALM 96:1

I got laid off from my job again. My agency lost its biggest client and laid off half its employees a few weeks before Christmas and after David and I bought a new house. So I'm job hunting, trying to finish this book, and over the holidays gained five pounds. But today, the sun is out and I will take a shower, washing off the disappointment, shame, gluttony, and fear. Instead, I hope for a new job that's a better fit than the last one. I hope for many years and memories in this new house. I hope for the discipline to stick to healthy eating so my body feels better. Believing in Christ's Resurrection means that from small, everyday deaths, we can have hope for new life. Tomorrow, I will sing a new song.

1 John 2:18–21
Psalm 96:1–2,11–12,13
John 1:1–18

Introduction

The little country church where I grew up smelled of old wood, Pledge, and flowers. I spent many hours of my childhood squirming in the pews, listening to sermons, and singing hymns like "How Great Thou Art," "Just as I Am," and "Amazing Grace."

We were Baptist, so our church services didn't follow the lectionary, but we still held the Scripture in the highest esteem. We memorized one verse a week and recited it during Sunday school. In youth group, we had "sword drills," where we raced to see who could find a verse in the Bible the fastest. We carried our Bibles to church for every service and opened them at night before bed to study during "quiet time." The strength of our faith was measured by our knowledge and understanding of Scripture. We dissected it, annotated it, read commentaries about it, trying to understand each verse and word. The problem was, Scripture was viewed as a textbook to be studied, not as a story to be lived.

As I grew older, the legalism of my childhood faith was too small, too confining, too static. The reality of my life

needed a bigger kind of faith. One that didn't have all the answers. One that included mystery—and grace.

For years, I didn't read the Bible. But when I became Catholic and started attending Mass, I would weep when I heard Scripture read during the liturgy. I felt like I had come home again, only this time Scripture wasn't a dry textbook. It was a living, breathing story filled with mystery and beauty, and a balm to my weary soul. Catholics didn't carry Bibles to church, but Scripture was the scaffolding that held up the entire Mass. I came to love the rhythms of the readings, the way we all stood and the priest lifted the lectionary high in the air before the Gospel reading. Going to Mass was (and still is!) like being invited to a feast where I am filled up each week, receiving the strength for the week ahead.

As I wrote the reflections in this book, I was struck by how certain themes emerge in the Bible—particularly how many times there are stories of banquets, dinners, and feasts, and how Jesus talks about himself as the bread of life. Much to the chagrin of the Jewish leaders, Jesus ate with tax collectors and prostitutes. Jesus didn't come to help people who were perfect. He came to heal the sick. And all he wants from us is to come and eat dinner with him.

When you read this book, think of it as a feast that God has prepared for you. Come to the banquet table just as you

are—whether you are tired, lonely, sad, scared, a sinner, or, sometimes, a doubter. Come to the table with the rest of us who are in the same shape, or worse off. The table is set, the wine has been poured, the guests are all seated, and Jesus is ready to break the bread.

Come, eat. Be filled.

No ear has ever heard, no eye ever seen,
any God but you
doing such deeds for those who wait for him.
—ISAIAH 64:3

And so it begins. The season of Advent when we remember
Christ's first coming and wait with hope for his second. We
are not good at waiting. It feels like nothing is happening.
We get bored and restless. But God is at work preparing our
hearts. And it's our job to be quiet and still so we can discern
what God is doing and recognize him when he arrives. Like
the shepherds keeping watch by night, and the wise men
gazing at the stars, we wait expectantly, contemplatively,
patiently for what God is about to do.

Isaiah 63:16b–17,19b; 64:2–7
Psalm 80:2–3,15–16,18–19
1 Corinthians 1:3–9
Mark 13:33–37

⇒ 1 ⇐

DECEMBER 4

• ST. JOHN DAMASCENE, PRIEST AND DOCTOR OF THE CHURCH •

"I say to you, many will come from the east and the west, and will recline with Abraham, Isaac, and Jacob at the banquet in the Kingdom of heaven."
—MATTHEW 8:11

One of my favorite movies is *Pieces of April*, an obscure, low-budget film from 2003. April is the oldest daughter of a highly dysfunctional family, including her mother, who has breast cancer. Although estranged from her somewhat crazy family, she invites them over to her small apartment on the Lower East Side for Thanksgiving dinner. Things go awry when she realizes her oven does not work, and so she has to reach out to other tenants in her building to help her cook the meal. The movie is a beautiful (and funny) portrayal of an eclectic and crazy group of people who gather together and experience grace, community, and healing—a small snapshot of the banquet in the kingdom of heaven.

Isaiah 2:1–5
Psalm 122:1–2,3–4b,4cd–5,6–7,8–9
Matthew 8:5–11

DECEMBER 5

"I give you praise, Father, Lord of heaven and earth, for although you have hidden these things from the wise and the learned you have revealed them to the childlike."
—LUKE 10:21

My daughter and I recently watched *The Little Prince* on Netflix, based on the novella by Antoine de Saint-Exupéry. It's the story of a pilot who is stranded in the desert, where he encounters the little prince, a boy who dispenses wisdom such as "One sees clearly only with the heart. What is essential is invisible to the eyes." And: "All grown-ups were once children . . . but only few of them remember it." When we grow up, the little prince believes, we lose much of that wonder and belief. Instead we get busy making money, becoming successful, trudging through modern-day life and all its struggles. We grow in Christ by becoming more like what we were at the beginning.

Isaiah 11:1–10
Psalm 72:1–2,7–8,12–13,17
Luke 10:21–24

The LORD is my shepherd;
I shall not want.
In verdant pastures, he gives me repose;
Beside restful waters he leads me;
he refreshes my soul.
—PSALM 23:1–3

I get angry with my daughter when I have to remind her—for the tenth time—to put on her shoes in the morning. I get frustrated with her inability to keep her room clean. I sometimes clean the kitchen instead of obliging her request to cuddle on the couch. And I often feel like a failure as a parent. But the other night I was reading a children's version of Psalm 23 to my daughter, and after putting the book down, she said, "Mommy, that book almost made me cry. You love me like that." It's the best compliment she could have given me. To let Jesus love us, and to love others as Jesus does. Isn't that what it's all about?

Isaiah 25:6–10a
Psalm 23:1–3a,3b–4,5,6
Matthew 15:29–37

"Not everyone who says to me, 'Lord, Lord,' will enter the Kingdom of heaven, but only the one who does the will of my Father in heaven."
—MATTHEW 7:21

We go to Mass, go through the motions, say and do all the right things. But it's much harder to submit to God's will.

That would mean we would have to give up our own agendas, our own plans. Not everyone is willing to do that, which is why Jesus says in Matthew 7:13 that we "enter through the narrow gate." We are standing at the gate. Will you enter with me?

Isaiah 26:1–6
Psalm 118:1 and 8–9,19–21,25–27a
Matthew 7:21,24–27

• THE IMMACULATE CONCEPTION OF THE BLESSED VIRGIN MARY (PATRONAL
FEASTDAY OF THE UNITED STATES OF AMERICA) •

In love he destined us for adoption to himself through Jesus Christ.
—EPHESIANS 1:4–5

My sister Sara spent a year teaching English in China in the 1980s. At the time, each family could only have one child in order to control the population. Since many couples wanted boys, female babies were often abandoned. My sister was determined to adopt one of these girls, and she did a few years later. This inspired my other sister, Ann, to adopt a girl from the same orphanage. Years later, my husband and I adopted our daughter, Desta, through foster care. That's why I often cry when I read about adopted children who find their "forever home." We have found our forever home in God. We are his—and as an adoptive parent, I know how much he must love each and every one of us.

Genesis 3:9–15,20
Psalm 98:1,2–3ab,3cd–4
Ephesians 1:3–6,11–12
Luke 1:26–38

Saturday

DECEMBER 9

• ST. JUAN DIEGO CUAUHTLATOATZIN •

While from behind, a voice shall sound in your ears:
"This is the way; walk in it,"
when you would turn to the right or to the left.
—ISAIAH 30:21

Many of us may hate making decisions, so having God behind us, whispering in our ear and telling us which direction to go, sounds great. But it takes practice to recognize his voice. In *The Sacred Journey*, Frederick Buechner writes, "There is no chance thing through which God cannot speak—even the walk from the house to the garage that you have walked ten thousand times before, even the moments when you cannot believe there is a God who speaks at all anywhere. He speaks, I believe, and the words he speaks are incarnate in the flesh and blood of our selves and of our own footsore and sacred journeys." Listen to your life and you will hear God.

Isaiah 30:19–21,23–26
Psalm 147:1–2,3–4,5–6
Matthew 9:35—10:1,5a,6–8

———————————

⇒ 7 ⇐

Sunday

DECEMBER 10

• SECOND SUNDAY OF ADVENT •

Make straight in the wasteland a highway for our God!
—ISAIAH 40:3

The word *Advent* is derived from the Latin *adventus*, which means "arrival" or "approach." Today we light another candle in the Advent wreath to prepare for Christ's coming. Like parents who are waiting for the arrival of their first child and clean out the boxes from the extra bedroom to turn it into a nursery, we clean out the unnecessary things in our lives to make room for Christ to enter. As you journey through this season, be silent, pray, light the candle, listen to Advent music, confess, give alms. Make straight in the wasteland a highway for our God.

Isaiah 40:1–5,9–11
Psalm 85:9–10,11–12,13–14
2 Peter 3:8–14
Mark 1:1–8

⇌ 8 ⇋

Then will the eyes of the blind be opened,
the ears of the deaf be cleared;
Then will the lame leap like a stag,
then the tongue of the mute will sing.
—ISAIAH 35:6

Oh, we wait for the day when the blind will see, the deaf will hear, the sick will be cured, the sad will rejoice, the exhausted will find rest, the downtrodden will be lifted up, the abused will find justice, the anxious will find peace, the lonely will feel loved, the invisible will be seen, the abandoned will find home, the old will be made new. We wait with hope.

Isaiah 35:1–10
Psalm 85:9ab and 10,11–12,13–14
Luke 5:17–26

DECEMBER 12

• OUR LADY OF GUADALUPE •

"Hail, full of grace! The Lord is with you."
—LUKE 1:28

The Lord is with us in that scary place, when we don't know
what's going on but we know we need to follow him. He's
with us even when we can't hear his voice. He's with us when
everyone else thinks we're crazy but we know we need to be
true to our calling. He's with us when we doubt. He's with us
when others gossip about us. He's with us when there is no
room at the inn. He's with us when we are grieving and when
we are joyful. He's with us when we are lonely. He's with us
when we bring new life into the world, in whatever form that
may take. God is with us, always.

Zechariah 2:14–17 or
Revelation 11:19a; 12:1–6a,10ab
Judith 13:18bcde,19
Luke 1:26–38 or 1:39–47

Wednesday

DECEMBER 13

• ST. LUCY, VIRGIN AND MARTYR •

"Come to me, all you who labor and are burdened, and I will give you rest."
—MATTHEW 11:28

In today's rat-race world, we work and work and work. Employers expect longer hours for less pay, and we are tethered to smartphones, answering e-mails at all times of the day and night. We want to quit the race, but how can we do that and still feed our families and pay our mortgages? And so we worry and lose sleep and keep working. Jesus said we can come to him and learn from him. He is meek and humble of heart. In him we can find rest. Today, Lord, help us find rest in you.

Isaiah 40:25–31
Psalm 103:1–2,3–4,8 and 10
Matthew 11:28–30

I am the LORD, your God,
who grasp your right hand;
It is I who say to you, "Fear not,
I will help you."
—ISAIAH 41:13

One night Desta ran into the living room. "Mommy, I want to tell you something, but I'm afraid." Tears ran down her cheeks. "Just tell me, honey, it's okay," I said. I took her hand. "No, I'm afraid you will be mad at me." I tried to guess the trouble—did she break something? No. Did she spill something? No. Did something happen to Binky? Yes. We ran upstairs and found her goldfish lying on the hardwood floor of her bedroom. I scooped him up and put him in his tank. Soon he was swimming again, a little stunned, but alive. When we do something wrong, when we are in trouble, when we are afraid, God will take our hand and rescue us, too.

Isaiah 41:13–20
Psalm 145:1 and 9,10–11,12–13ab
Matthew 11:11–15

*"'Look, he is a glutton and a drunkard, a friend of tax collectors
and sinners.' But wisdom is vindicated by her works."*
—MATTHEW 11:19

Jesus chides the crowd for not recognizing him in their
midst—and for judging him for eating and drinking with tax
collectors and sinners. On the other hand, the crowd also
judged John the Baptist for not eating and drinking. They
said he was possessed by a demon. So there was no way to
please this crowd. In reality, the people probably just didn't
want to face and acknowledge the message of Good News
that John and Jesus were preaching. We too may focus on the
wrong things in order to avoid the one truth we really need
to face, especially when we are too comfortable, too afraid,
or too set in our ways. But Jesus reminds us that the truth will
set us free.

Isaiah 48:17–19
Psalm 1:1–2,3,4 and 6
Matthew 11:16–19

DECEMBER 16

In those days,
like a fire there appeared the prophet Elijah
whose words were as a flaming furnace.
—SIRACH 48:1

The great prophet Elijah, whose name means "My God is Yahweh," defended Yahweh against those who worshipped the idol Baal. His words were "as a flaming furnace," he raised the dead, brought fire from the sky, and was taken up in a whirlwind of fire. Apparently, he was a force to be reckoned with. I wonder, how can we be a force to be reckoned with in this world? How can our words be a flaming furnace—passionate enough for God to use them to turn others away from their idols?

Sirach 48:1–4,9–11
Psalm 80:2ac and 3b,15–16,18–19
Matthew 17:9a,10–13

DECEMBER 17

• THIRD SUNDAY OF ADVENT •

Rejoice always. Pray without ceasing. In all circumstances give thanks,
for this is the will of God for you in Christ Jesus.
—1 THESSALONIANS 5:16–18

With every breath, God, you are here beside me. I sense your
presence. Throughout the day, I am aware of you. In my
work, my conversations, my seemingly mundane tasks. Also,
when I rise and when I go to bed. I know you are with me. I
praise you and thank you. I talk to you without ceasing, for
you are the one who sustains me.

Isaiah 61:1–2a,10–11
Luke 1:46–48,49–50,53–54
1 Thessalonians 5:16–24
John 1:6–8,19–28

DECEMBER 18

"God is with us."
—MATTHEW 1:23

These days, you hear a lot about "being present." This can mean being fully present in the moment, or being physically present and attentive to whomever you are with. The Zen poet and peace activist Thich Nhat Hanh says, "The most precious gift we can offer others is our presence. When mindfulness embraces those we love, they will bloom like flowers." Just sitting with someone in pain can mean the world to that person. God offered his presence to us through his son, Jesus Christ, who sits with us in our pain and helps us bloom.

Jeremiah 23:5–8
Psalm 72:1–2,12–13,18–19
Matthew 1:18–25

DECEMBER 19

An angel of the LORD appeared to the woman and said to her, "Though you are barren and have had no children, yet you will conceive and bear a son."
—JUDGES 13:3

Three times in Scripture, an angel appears to a woman and tells her she is going to conceive. I'm struck by the reactions of these three women: Monoah's wife (she is unnamed in the Bible) was calm, even though her husband, Monoah, freaked out. Elizabeth was joyful and grateful to God, even though her husband, Zechariah, questioned God and didn't believe that she could conceive, so God struck him mute. And Mary was open and accepting, as Joseph stewed about how this could happen and contemplated a divorce. Maybe God used these women to bring the Good News into the world because they were courageous, open, and calm—and they trusted him.

Judges 13:2–7,24–25a
Psalm 71:3–4a,5–6ab,16–17
Luke 1:5–25

DECEMBER 20

Ask for a sign from the LORD, your God; let it be deep as the nether world, or high as the sky!
—ISAIAH 7:11

Once, I lost my work parking space and knew it was a sign from God. My job was in the city, where parking is expensive, but I rented a spot that was convenient and cheap. One day I learned that my coveted parking contract was not being renewed, and I wondered if God was trying to tell me something. The next day, my company announced we had lost our biggest client. Half of the employees were laid off, including me. But I wasn't too disappointed. I had been unhappy with my job for a while, and now I had the chance to find a job where I could better use my gifts. Sometimes signs come in odd ways, but we know God is up to something good.

Isaiah 7:10–14
Psalm 24:1–2,3–4ab,5–6
Luke 1:26–38

DECEMBER 21

• ST. PETER CANISIUS, PRIEST AND DOCTOR OF THE CHURCH •

The King of Israel, the LORD, is in your midst,
you have no further misfortune to fear.
—ZEPHANIAH 3:15

Fear makes us do crazy things. We take jobs we don't want because we're afraid of financial insecurity. We rush into marriage because we're afraid of being alone. On the other hand, we may become workaholics because we're afraid of failure. We may lead a lonely life because we're afraid of intimacy. It's easy to understand why Scripture often tells us not to be afraid. Fear does little but stunt our growth and our joy. Fear is a failure to trust that no matter what happens, God is working everything together for good in our lives. Instead, we should follow the example of Job, who said, "Slay me though he might, I will wait for him." (NAB Job 13:15)

Song of Songs 2:8–14 or
Zephaniah 3:14–18a
Psalm 33:2–3,11–12,20–21
Luke 1:39–45

⇒ 19 ⇐

"I prayed for this child, and the LORD granted my request. Now I, in turn, give him to the LORD; as long as he lives, he shall be dedicated to the LORD." She left Samuel there.

—1 SAMUEL 1:27–28

How hard it must have been for Hannah to give Samuel to the Lord. In gratitude to God for answering her prayer for a child, she left Samuel in the temple in Shiloh so he could be used by God. It's hard for parents to realize that their children are not their own. They are a gift from God, and at some point, we must let them go. All gifts we have belong to God. How are you giving your gifts back to God for his use?

1 Samuel 1:24–28
1 Samuel 2:1,4–5,6–7,8abcd
Luke 1:46–56

DECEMBER 23

• ST. JOHN OF KANTY, PRIEST •

Immediately his mouth was opened, his tongue freed.
—LUKE 1:64

Zechariah is struck mute because he questions the message
from the angel that his wife, Elizabeth, is pregnant in her old
age. But he gets a second chance. On the eighth day after his
son's birth, when it's time to name the baby and all the
relatives are gathered around, Elizabeth announces that the
baby will be called John in obedience to God. Their relatives
are incredulous. Didn't they want to name the baby
Zechariah after his father? So they turn to Zechariah for his
opinion. Still mute, he writes on a tablet: "John is his name."
Immediately, his tongue is freed and he is able to talk. When
we follow and trust God, we too will be free.

Malachi 3:1–4,23–24
Psalm 25:4–5ab,8–9,10 and 14
Luke 1:57–66

DECEMBER 24

"And of his kingdom there will be no end."
—LUKE 1:33

When I was young, my family would celebrate Christmas Eve with my mother's side of the family. We would all gather at my grandparents' house for our traditional Swedish meal of lutefisk, limpa bread, rice pudding, and potato sausage. We would read the Christmas story, and each child would unwrap one present. Then we would go home and go to bed, waiting with anticipation for Christmas morning when we would unwrap the rest of our gifts. Now that I'm older and Catholic, David, Desta, and I attend Christmas Eve Mass together. If we have dinner with extended family, we eat ham instead of lutefisk. However our traditions may change, tonight is still when we wait in prayerful anticipation for Christ's birth in our lives and for the coming of his kingdom for which there will be no end.

2 Samuel 7:1–5,8b–12,14a,16
Psalm 89:2–3,4–5,27,29 (2a)
Romans 16:25–27
Luke 1:26–38

DECEMBER 25

• THE NATIVITY OF THE LORD (CHRISTMAS) •

In the beginning was the Word,
and the Word was with God,
and the Word was God.
—JOHN 1:1

Throughout the ages we have strung words together to make stories, to mediate the thoughts from one person to the other. "Word" comes from the Greek *logos*, which was thought of as a bridge between the transcendent God and the material universe. So "the Word" was a window through which God was making himself known to us. Through this Word made flesh that we celebrate today begins the greatest story ever told.

VIGIL:
Isaiah 62:1–5
Psalm 89:4–5,16–17,27,29 (2a)
Acts 13:16–17,22–25
Matthew 1:1–25 or 1:18–25

NIGHT:
Isaiah 9:1–6
Psalm 96:1–2,2–3,11–12,13
Titus 2:11–14
Luke 2:1–14

DAWN:
Isaiah 62:11–12
Psalm 97:1,6,11–12
Titus 3:4–7
Luke 2:15–20

DAY:
Isaiah 52:7–10
Psalm 98:1,2–3,3–4,5–6 (3c)
Hebrews 1:1–6
John 1:1–18

DECEMBER 26

• ST. STEPHEN, THE FIRST MARTYR •

But he, filled with the Holy Spirit, looked up intently to heaven.
—ACTS 6:8

Ever since she was little, Desta has loved looking at the sky at night. One night, when she was only about three, long after I thought she was asleep, she called from her room, "Mommy, Mommy, come here!" Annoyed that she was still awake, I stomped into her room to scold her. But as I entered, she said excitedly, "Mommy, the moon, the moon!" I looked out the window, and the full moon was shining as bright as I'd ever seen it. We both stood there in awe. We look to the heavens to be inspired, to seek God, to admire his creation. Psalm 121:1–2 says, "I raise my eyes toward the mountains. / From whence shall come my help? / My help comes from the LORD, / the maker of heaven and earth."

Acts 6:8–10; 7:54–59
Psalm 31:3cd–4,6 and 8ab,16bc and 17
Matthew 10:17–22

DECEMBER 27

• ST. JOHN, APOSTLE AND EVANGELIST •

We are writing this so that our joy may be complete.
—1 JOHN 1:4

We try and try to make ourselves completely happy. We think we can do it, but there's always something missing. We think, *If I only finish school and get a job, then I'll be happy.* Or, *Once I get married, my life will be complete.* Or, *When I have children, I will be perfectly content.* And yet once we get all those things, we still yearn for something else, something more. Only when we look to the baby in the manger will our constant longings fade. Only when we look to the baby in the manger will our joy be complete.

1 John 1:1–4
Psalm 97:1–2,5–6,11–12
John 20:1a and 2–8

But if we walk in the light as he is in the light, then we have fellowship with one another.

—1 JOHN 1:7

There's nothing like having community with other believers. When we are following God, there is a spirit of unity, grace, love. But when we are walking in sin, we are kept not only from God but also from our friends and family. What is keeping you from having fellowship with those around you?

1 John 1:5—2:2
Psalm 124:2–3,4–5,7b–8
Matthew 2:13–18

Whoever says he is in the light, yet hates his brother, is still in the darkness.

—1 JOHN 2:9

Martin Luther King Jr. said, "Darkness cannot drive out darkness: only light can do that. Hate cannot drive out hate: only love can do that." I live not far from where King staged the Chicago Freedom Movement and marched fifty years ago against unfair housing practices in Chicago that discriminated against blacks. I get discouraged when I think about the discrimination that still exists in my city, half a century later. Then I ask myself, how am I being a light in the darkness?

1 John 2:3–11
Psalm 96:1–2a,2b–3,5b–6
Luke 2:22–35

DECEMBER 30

• SIXTH DAY WITHIN THE OCTAVE OF THE NATIVITY OF THE LORD •

Yet the world and its enticement are passing away. But whoever does the will of God remains forever.

—1 JOHN 2:17

We get enticed by the glittering, dazzling Las Vegas lights of the world. The carnies luring us into the sideshow tents. The Mad men advertisers selling us the beautiful life. But it is all passing. All of it. When will we learn? Simone Weil, in her book *Waiting for God*, says, "Sin is not a distance, it is a turning of our gaze in the wrong direction."

1 John 2:12–17
Psalm 96:7–8a,8b–9,10
Luke 2:36–40

DECEMBER 31

• THE HOLY FAMILY OF JESUS, MARY, AND JOSEPH •

By faith Abraham obeyed when he was called to go out to a place that he was to receive as an inheritance; he went out, not knowing where he was to go.

—HEBREWS 11:8

Where is God calling you? Do you hear his call? Can you take one step in that direction, even if you don't know where you're supposed to go or how things will turn out? Follow the example of Abraham and Mary and Joseph. They all responded to God's call, despite their fear, and took the first tiny, tentative step.

Genesis 15:1–6; 21:1–3 or
Sirach 3:2–6,12–14
Psalm 105:1–2,3–4,5–6,8–9 or
Psalm 128:1–2,3,4–5
Hebrews 11:8,11–12,17–19 or
Colossians 3:12–21 or 3:12–17
Luke 2:22–40 or 2:22,39–40

JANUARY 1

• THE SOLEMNITY OF MARY, THE HOLY MOTHER OF GOD •

And Mary kept all these things, reflecting on them in her heart.
—LUKE 2:19

Did Mary understand what was happening? Did she realize that her baby would change the whole world? She must have been confused by the events, and yet she kept her questions in her heart and pondered them. She wasn't skeptical. She didn't reject the messages from the angels. She kept an open mind and heart and waited, reflected, accepted. May we all be like Mary.

Numbers 6:22–27
Psalm 67:2–3,5,6,8
Galatians 4:4–7
Luke 2:16–21

> "*I am* the voice of one crying out in the desert,
> 'Make straight the way of the Lord.'"
> —JOHN 1:23

The Catholic novelist Flannery O'Connor is known for
creating freakish characters in her novels. She once said, "You
shall know the truth and the truth shall make you odd." John
the Baptist was one such odd character who could have
appeared in a Flannery O'Connor novel. He wore clothes
made of camel's hair and lived on locusts and wild honey. But
he had an important purpose to fulfill: to announce Christ's
coming and to prepare the way. Maybe a freakish character
like John the Baptist was the perfect messenger to shake
people out of their complacency and let them know that
Christ was coming to turn their world upside down.
Sometimes we have to be shaken out of our everyday lives to
be open to letting Christ change us.

1 John 2:22–28
Psalm 98:1,2–3ab,3cd–4
John 1:19–28

Wednesday

JANUARY 3

• THE MOST HOLY NAME OF JESUS •

Beloved, we are God's children now; what we shall be has not yet been revealed. We do know that when it is revealed we shall be like him, for we shall see him as he is.

—1 JOHN 3:2

We are living in the "now," the "not yet." Christ's kingdom is here, but it is not yet fully realized. How frustrating it can be to live in that tension. We know Christ is working in our lives and in the world, to heal, restore, and save us. And yet we still see and experience so much brokenness, heartache, and pain. It's easy to lose hope. But remember, we are still in the middle of the story. The last chapter has not yet been written. It will be epic.

1 John 2:29—3:6
Psalm 98:1,3cd—4,5–6
John 1:29–34

Thursday

JANUARY 4

Sing to the LORD a new song,
for he has done wondrous deeds;
His right hand has won victory for him,
his holy arm.
—PSALM 98:1

I have a trunk filled with old journals, and I often reread them. I'm astonished to see what I was writing about, praying about, pleading with God about, five, ten, fifteen years ago. God has since answered many of my prayers and changed the things that I begged him to change in my life. The pain of waiting is now just a faint memory. But how many times have I thanked God for answering those prayers? It's so easy to forget what the Lord has done in our lives. The psalmist reminds us today that God has done wondrous deeds. And my song of lament has turned into a song of praise.

1 John 3:7–10
Psalm 98:1,7–8,9
John 1:35–42

Friday

JANUARY 5

• ST. JOHN NEUMANN, BISHOP •

The way we came to know love was that he laid down his life for us; so
we ought to lay down our lives for our brothers.
—1 JOHN 3:16

I always heard that you never realize how selfish you are
until you get married. I have found this to be true. Each
partner must sacrifice something for the other. I worked at a
job I didn't like so that my husband could go back to school.
My husband has given up his time and freedom to take care
of our daughter so that I can attend writing conferences. We
give up something so that those we love can thrive. And now
that we have a daughter, we sacrifice our time, energy, and
resources for her every day. By laying down our lives for
another—following Christ's example—we come to
understand true love.

1 John 3:11–21
Psalm 100:1b–2,3,4,5
John 1:43–51

JANUARY 6

• ST. ANDRÉ BESSETTE, RELIGIOUS •

This is the one who came through water and Blood, Jesus Christ, not by
water alone, but by water and Blood.
—1 JOHN 5:6

Scholars disagree as to what it means that Jesus came through water and blood. It could refer to his death, when the soldier put a spear through his side and out came water and blood. It could also mean his birth, when he was born to Mary. Everyone who has given birth or has observed a birth knows that there is water and blood involved. But whatever it means, this passage attests to Christ's humanity. He was both divine and human. It's hard to get our heads around that. But whenever we go through any kind of suffering, it's immensely comforting to know that Christ bled just as we bleed, that he was truly one of us and knows our pain.

1 John 5:5–13
Psalm 147:12–13,14–15,19–20
Mark 1:7–11 or Luke 3:23–38 or
3:23,31–34,36,38

*"Where is the newborn king of the Jews? We saw his star at its rising
and have come to do him homage."*
—MATTHEW 2:2

Would you have noticed the star in the sky? Or would you
have been too busy and distracted? Would you have been
quiet and still enough to look up, to contemplate the stars
and the greatness of the universe? To stop and be in awe? To
breathe in the cold night air? To notice that something was
happening? Sometimes we wait for God to come, but what
we really need to do is be quiet and attentive enough to
notice and discern what he is already doing. And more often
than not, God is found where we least expect him.

Isaiah 60:1–6
Psalm 72:1–2,7–8,10–11,12–13
Ephesians 3:2–3a,5–6
Matthew 2:1–12

JANUARY 8

• THE BAPTISM OF THE LORD •

And a voice came from the heavens, "You are my beloved Son; with you
I am well pleased."
—MARK 1:11

The poet Raymond Carver writes: "And did you get what /
you wanted from this life, even so? / I did. / And what did
you want? / To call myself beloved, to feel myself /
beloved on the earth." That's what we all want, isn't it? To feel
beloved? We spend our days making ourselves more
"lovable," whether it's putting on makeup to feel attractive
and acceptable, or working long hours to become more
successful and admired, or giving up parts of ourselves to
please another person so they will love us. It's hard to
remember that we are God's beloved. And that nothing can
separate us from the love of God. He loves us just as we are.

Isaiah 42:1–4,6–7 or 55:1–11 or
Acts 10:34–38 or 1 John 5:1–9
Psalm 29:1–2,3–4,3,9–10 or
Isaiah 12:2–3,4bcd,5–6
Mark 1:7–11

Tuesday

JANUARY 9

He raises the needy from the dust;
from the dung heap he lifts up the poor,
To seat them with nobles
and make a glorious throne their heritage.
—1 SAMUEL 2:8

We live in a hierarchical world. People are ranked by their title, their status, the color of their skin, how much money they have, how big of a home they live in. But over and over again in Scripture, this hierarchy is flattened. The poor eat with the rich. The haughty are humbled. The mighty are broken. To be like Jesus, we need to view people differently—to see the rich and the homeless, the beautiful and the ordinary, the mayors and the janitors as all equally worthy of God's love and our love.

1 Samuel 1:9–20
1 Samuel 2:1,4–5,6–7,8abcd
Mark 1:21–28

JANUARY 10

"Speak, LORD, for your servant is listening."
—1 SAMUEL 3:10

Samuel heard God's voice three times, but he didn't realize that it was God. He thought it was Eli and said, "Here I am. You called me." Finally, when Eli told him it was God, Samuel answered, "Speak, for your servant is listening." Hearing God in the midst of our chaotic lives can be challenging. We might dismiss his call, be too busy to hear it, too afraid to answer it, or misunderstand it as something else. And yet, the young boy Samuel serves as an example: We need to say, "Here I am, your servant is listening."

1 Samuel 3:1–10,19–20
Psalm 40:2 and 5,7–8a,8b–9,10
Mark 1:29–39

JANUARY 11

A leper came to him and kneeling down begged him and said, "If you wish, you can make me clean." Moved with pity, he stretched out his hand, touched the leper, and said to him, "I do will it. Be made clean."
—MARK 1:40–41

There used to be a reality show called *Extreme Makeover*. The show's participants usually had some complaint about how they looked—a large nose, a receding hairline, a too-small chin—and they were transformed through plastic surgery, a new wardrobe, and a stylish haircut. At the end of each episode was the big reveal, where their family and friends gathered to see the transformed main character. The Christian life is like *Extreme Makeover*—only it's a transformation of the heart. God wants to transform and heal us. We only need to be like the leper and ask him to cure us and make us clean.

1 Samuel 4:1–11
Psalm 44:10–11,14–15,24–25
Mark 1:40–45

JANUARY 12

He said to the paralytic, "I say to you, rise, pick up your mat, and go
home." . . . They were all astounded and glorified God, saying, "We
have never seen anything like this."
—MARK 2:11–12

The writer Frederick Buechner said that "Coincidences are
God's way of getting our attention." In all my years as a
Christian, I have never seen God heal a leper. And yet I have
experienced small miracles—coincidences that I can only
explain as being works of God. For years, my husband and I
were trying to adopt a child from Ethiopia. We finally gave
up, and eventually adopted a toddler through foster care, a
little girl whose name was Destinee and whose former foster
family had nicknamed "Desta." We discovered that Desta is
an Ethiopian name that means "joy." Coincidence? Nah, I
choose to believe it was a miracle.

1 Samuel 8:4–7,10–22a
Psalm 89:16–17,18–19
Mark 2:1–12

JANUARY 13

· ST. HILARY, BISHOP AND DOCTOR OF THE CHURCH ·

Jesus said to him, "Follow me." And he got up and followed Jesus.
—MARK 2:14

What does it mean to follow Jesus? To get up and follow without hesitation? The disciples left everything behind, without hesitation, to follow Christ. Do we really believe that following Jesus is worth giving it all up? In his book *Radical*, author and pastor David Platt writes: "Do we really believe He is worth abandoning everything for? Do you and I really believe that Jesus is so good, so satisfying and so rewarding that we will leave all we have and all we own and all we are in order to find our fullness in Him? Do you and I believe Him enough to obey Him and to follow Him wherever He leads?"

1 Samuel 9:1–4,17–19; 10:1
Psalm 21:2–3,4–5,6–7
Mark 2:13–17

Sunday

JANUARY 14

• SECOND SUNDAY IN ORDINARY TIME •

Do you not know that your body is a temple of the Holy Spirit within you, whom you have from God, and that you are not your own? For you have been purchased at a price. Therefore glorify God in your body.
—1 CORINTHIANS 6:19–20

How would we treat our bodies differently if we truly believed that they were the temples of the Holy Spirit? Would we eat differently? Get off the couch and exercise more? Look at our cellulite and wrinkles in the mirror in a new way? If we believed that our bodies were not our own but belonged to our heavenly Father, would we treat our bodies as the precious vessels that they are?

1 Samuel 3:3b–10,19
Psalm 40:2,4,7–8,8–9,10 (8a,9a)
1 Corinthians 6:13c–15a,17–20
John 1:35–42

"Why do you recite my statutes,
and profess my covenant with your mouth,
Though you hate discipline
and cast my words behind you?"
—PSALM 50:16–17

How many times do I just pay lip service to my faith? I can
certainly talk the talk. I know the right words to say. I want
to look spiritual to others. But do my actions back up my
words? Do I actually do all the things I talk about? Lord, help
me follow you with my actions, not just with my words.

1 Samuel 15:16–23
Psalm 50:8–9,16bc–17,21 and 23
Mark 2:18–22

Tuesday

JANUARY 16

*"Not as man sees does God see, because he sees the appearance but the
LORD looks into the heart."*
—1 SAMUEL 16:7

I once heard someone say that beauty isn't determined by
how you look but by how you look at other people. Our
society is obsessed with physical beauty. I admit I size people
up by their appearance. How are they dressed? Do they fit
our culture's standards of beauty? Slowly, though, God has
been changing my perspective. I pray to see someone's inner
beauty first. And as I age and get wrinkles and gray hair, I
pray that others will see me as God sees me as well, by my
heart and not by my physical appearance.

1 Samuel 16:1–13
Psalm 89:20,21–22,27–28
Mark 2:23–28

They watched Jesus closely to see if he would cure him on the sabbath.
—MARK 3:2

The Hebrew word *sabat* means "to rest or stop or cease from work." I don't know about you, but I feel guilty when I have a day where I'm not doing much. I feel lazy. I feel like I should be working, or cleaning the house, or going grocery shopping, or folding laundry, or answering work e-mails. Especially since, when I do stop doing everything, I don't have any distractions to keep me from hearing my own thoughts, and that's scary. If we follow sabat, though, we know that it's okay to stop our constant work. And maybe that's the only way we will really hear God's voice.

1 Samuel 17:32–33,37,40–51
Psalm 144:1b,2,9–10
Mark 3:1–6

JANUARY 18

My adversaries trample upon me all the day;
yes, many fight against me.
My wanderings you have counted;
my tears are stored in your flask.
—PSALM 56:3,9

Do you ever feel like your adversaries are trampling you? How about that coworker who seems out to get you? Or the hostile family member who doesn't like your politics? Or the parent of your child's schoolmate who is upset that your child made the basketball team but hers didn't? Or even the driver who cut you off on your way to work? Some days it all feels like too much. But God cares about these everyday struggles, and he's storing your tears in his flask.

1 Samuel 18:6–9; 19:1–7
Psalm 56:2–3,9–10a,10b–11,12–13
Mark 3:7–12

"I had some thought of killing you, but I took pity on you instead."
—1 SAMUEL 24:11

Saul is hunting down David with an army of 3,000 because he is jealous of him. Saul stops into a cave to "relieve" himself, not knowing that David and his servants are hiding there. David has his chance to kill Saul to defend himself, but instead, he takes pity on him. What a beautiful picture of grace and redemption. David has all the reasons in the world to kill Saul so that he himself will not be murdered. But instead, he offers grace. At the end of the passage, David and Saul are both weeping and declaring their love and respect for each other. Today, offer grace to an enemy. Your act of mercy may be the thing that transforms your whole relationship.

1 Samuel 24:3–21
Psalm 57:2,3–4,6 and 11
Mark 3:13–19

Saturday

JANUARY 20

Jesus came with his disciples into the house. Again the crowd gathered,
making it impossible for them even to eat. When his relatives heard of this
they set out to seize him, for they said, "He is out of his mind."
—MARK 3:20–21

It must have been confusing for people in Jesus' day to
understand what he was all about. The miracles, the crowds
following him, his puzzling parables—he probably did seem
out of his mind. But those people had a choice: to see the
craziness or to see a Savior. Following Christ sometimes
means we may look foolish in the world's eyes. In his book
Mere Christianity, C. S. Lewis writes about Jesus, "You must
make your choice. Either this man was, and is, the Son of
God, or else a madman or something worse." I'm willing to
follow that madman. Are you?

2 Samuel 1:1–4,11–12,19,23–27
Psalm 80:2–3,5–7
Mark 3:20–21

JANUARY 21

• THIRD SUNDAY IN ORDINARY TIME •

I tell you, brothers and sisters, the time is running out.
—1 CORINTHIANS 7:29

Time haunts me. It passes so quickly through my hands that I
cannot grab hold of it long enough to do everything I want
to do. I waste time. Pass the time. Wish I had more of it. I
long for the day when time will be no more, and we will be
with Him forever.

Jonah 3:1–5,10
Psalm 25:4–5,6–7,8–9 (4a)
1 Corinthians 7:29–31
Mark 1:14–20

JANUARY 22

"I have found David, my servant;
with my holy oil I have anointed him,
That my hand may be always with him,
and that my arm may make him strong."
—PSALM 89:21–22

Throughout Scripture, oil is used to bless, heal, and anoint. During confirmation, the bishop presses oil into our forehead and says, "Be sealed with the gift of the Holy Spirit." When we adopted our black daughter, I had no idea how to take care of her hair. I learned that black hair gets dry, and taking care of it is time-consuming. I started resenting the hours it took to moisturize and braid it. But then I realized how precious this time with my daughter is, and now when I take olive oil and rub it into her scalp, I pray that she will be safe and strong and sealed with the gift of the Holy Spirit.

2 Samuel 5:1–7,10
Psalm 89:20,21–22,25–26
Mark 3:22–30

Tuesday

JANUARY 23

• ST. MARIANNE COPE, VIRGIN • ST. VINCENT OF SARAGOSSA, DEACON AND MARTYR •

"Your mother and your brothers and your sisters are outside asking for you." But he said to them in reply, "Who are my mother and my brothers?" And looking around at those seated in the circle he said, "Here are my mother and my brothers. For whoever does the will of God is my brother and sister and mother."

—MARK 3:31–35

Ouch. That must have stung Jesus' family when he publicly blew them off. But the fact was that Jesus' mission required his loyalties to shift. He was no longer just a member of his nuclear family. He was part of his spiritual family. Sometimes it's hard to break away from the expectations of our families. We love them and don't want to disappoint them. But when it comes to doing our family's will or God's will, we have to make a choice.

2 Samuel 6:12b–15,17–19
Psalm 24:7,8,9,10
Mark 3:31–35

"And some seed fell on rich soil and produced fruit. It came up and grew and yielded thirty, sixty, and a hundredfold."
—MARK 4:8

My Scottish ancestors settled on the prairies of Iowa in 1864, where they grew corn for over a century in the black, soft soil—the most fertile ground in the world. Soil, the top layer of earth, consists of old plants and leaves and fallen debris that worms and fungi have broken down into nutritious organic matter. Basically, soil is made up of dead things that have been broken, and these dead, broken things offer a foundation for new life. As a child, I remember the smell of the Iowa earth in the spring—musty, clean, ancient. It would be years before I would understand that from brokenness and loss so much fruit would come.

2 Samuel 7:4–17
Psalm 89:4–5,27–28,29–30
Mark 4:1–20

Thursday

JANUARY 25

• THE CONVERSION OF ST. PAUL THE APOSTLE •

"On that journey as I drew near to Damascus, about noon a great light from the sky suddenly shone around me."
—ACTS 22:6

Sometimes conversions, like Paul's, are sudden and dramatic. Paul saw a great light and fell to the ground and heard God's voice. Those conversions make great stories, and we love to hear them. In my childhood Baptist church, these were the testimonies that brought the most "Amens!" in the Sunday night service. But most times, conversions are a slow turning toward the light, like a morning glory opening her petals to the warm sun. Either way, whether we are blinded by the light or turning slowly toward it, the light can change us forever.

Acts 22:3–16 or 9:1–22
Psalm 117:1bc,2
Mark 16:15–18

⇒ 54 ⇐

Friday

JANUARY 26

• SS. TIMOTHY AND TITUS, BISHOPS •

For God did not give us a spirit of cowardice but rather of power and love and self-control.
—2 TIMOTHY 1:7

I have never thought of love as being the opposite of cowardice. But it makes sense. When we lack courage to reach out, to use our gifts, to be the person God created us to be, we hold back what those around us need the most. It takes courage to love others. When we "put ourselves out there," we risk being rejected or hurt. But it's only when we are giving our whole selves to others that we are truly loving them.

2 Timothy 1:1–8 or Titus 1:1–5
Psalm 96:1–2a,2b–3,7–8a,10
Mark 4:26–34

JANUARY 27

• ST. ANGELA MERICI, VIRGIN •

He woke up, rebuked the wind, and said to the sea, "Quiet! Be still!"
—MARK 4:39

When you feel like you're in a boat that's filling with water in
the middle of a storm and you're afraid, be still. Listen for
God's voice. Have faith. "The silence," says the poet Rumi,
"gives answers."

2 Samuel 12:1–7a,10–17
Psalm 51:12–13,14–15,16–17
Mark 4:35–41

Sunday

JANUARY 28

• FOURTH SUNDAY IN ORDINARY TIME •

Brothers and sisters: I should like you to be free of anxieties.
—1 CORINTHIANS 7:32

Throughout Scripture, we are told to "have no anxiety at all" (Philippians 4:6), "not worry about tomorrow" (Matthew 6:34), and that "worry weighs down the heart." (Proverbs 12:25) Easier said than done. I suffer from an anxiety disorder, and these commands are difficult for me. Anxiety has paralyzed me, affected my relationships, and held me back in my career. I sometimes take medication for it, but I also know that when I feel closer to God, it's easier for me to trust that everything will be OK.

Deuteronomy 18:15–20
Psalm 95:1–2,6–7,7–9 (8)
1 Corinthians 7:32–35
Mark 1:21–28

Catching sight of Jesus from a distance, he ran up and prostrated himself before him, crying out in a loud voice, "What have you to do with me, Jesus, Son of the Most High God?"
—MARK 5:6–7

Why do you want anything to do with me, God? I yell at my kid; I fail to love my husband. I procrastinate, I'm a coward, I don't return text messages from my friends. I haven't visited my ailing father in six months. Every time you give me what I want, I forget to thank you for it. I ignore you and then blame you for my lot in life. Why don't you just give up on me? I sit in silence, and God answers me in his response to the demon-possessed man: "Go home to your family and announce to them all that the Lord in his pity has done for you."

2 Samuel 15:13–14,30; 16:5–13
Psalm 3:2–3,4–5,6–7
Mark 5:1–20

Tuesday

JANUARY 30

"Daughter, your faith has saved you. Go in peace and be cured of your affliction."
—MARK 5:34

The woman had been afflicted by hemorrhaging for twelve years. Twelve long years. And yet the bleeding woman had hope that if she could just touch the hem of Jesus' coat, she would be healed. Our afflictions can feel like they last forever with no end in sight. But this passage reminds us that there is always the hope of healing. This woman waited twelve years. How long have you been waiting?

2 Samuel 18:9–10,14b,24–25a,30—19:3
Psalm 86:1–2,3–4,5–6
Mark 5:21–43

Then I acknowledged my sin to you,
my guilt I covered not.
I said, "I confess my faults to the LORD,
and you took away the guilt of my sin."
—PSALM 32:5

Confession gets a bad rap: Guilty churchgoers in confession booths has been the subject of more than one comedy scene in a movie. Before I became Catholic, I confessed my sin silently—in prayer to God. But during my first sacrament of reconciliation as a Catholic, I learned how powerful it is to confess your sins aloud to another person. Giving voice to our sin brings it into the light, where it cannot be hidden and rot. And hearing another person speak God's forgiveness to you feels like someone is physically lifting the burden from you and removing any barrier that is keeping you from the loving embrace of God.

2 Samuel 24:2,9–17
Psalm 32:1–2,5,6,7
Mark 6:1–6

FEBRUARY 1

He instructed them to take nothing for the journey but a walking stick—no food, no sack, no money in their belts. They were, however, to wear sandals but not a second tunic.
—MARK 6:8–9

When I travel, I pack like I'm going to be gone for years. I want to be prepared for every scenario. My husband, on the other hand, grabs a duffle bag and puts in a few shirts and a pair of jeans and he's good to go. I've tried to learn from him.

You can travel faster with a lighter suitcase—no need to check your bag, and it's easier to walk through the airport. There are many advantages to packing light. Jesus needed his disciples to be quick, agile, and unburdened to do the work he was calling them to do. What do you need to let go of to follow Jesus' call?

1 Kings 2:1–4,10–12
1 Chronicles 29:10,11ab,11d–12a,12bcd
Mark 6:7–13

FEBRUARY 2

• THE PRESENTATION OF THE LORD •

"Now, Master, you may let your servant go
in peace, according to your word,
for my eyes have seen your salvation,
which you prepared in the sight
of all the peoples:
a light for revelation to the Gentiles,
and glory for your people Israel."
—LUKE 2:29–32

Simeon was waiting to see Christ. He had a revelation that
he would not die before seeing the Christ child, and so when
Mary and Joseph presented Jesus to God in Jerusalem forty
days after his birth, according to Jewish law, Simeon was
there in the temple. He knew this baby contained the hope
of the whole world. Are you waiting to see Christ today? Are
you waiting for hope?

Malachi 3:1–4
Psalm 24:7,8,9,10
Hebrews 2:14–18
Luke 2:22–40

FEBRUARY 3

• ST. BLAISE, BISHOP AND MARTYR • ST. ANSGAR, BISHOP •

*We even boast of our afflictions, knowing that affliction produces
endurance, and endurance, proven character, and proven character, hope,
and hope does not disappoint, because the love of God has been poured
into our hearts through the Holy Spirit that has been given to us.*
—ROMANS 5:3–5 (FROM FEAST DAY READING)

Sometimes you may feel like there is no path out of the dark
forest of pain. But eventually, you will see a small pinpoint of
light through the trees. And if you walk in that direction, a
path will appear. When you emerge from the trees, you will
know that you were strong enough to survive your affliction,
and your capacity for love will have expanded tenfold. In his
book *Everything Belongs*, Richard Rohr writes, "In terms of soul
work, we dare not get rid of the pain before we have learned
what it has to teach us."

1 Kings 3:4–13
Psalm 119:9,10,11,12,13,14
Mark 6:30–34

FEBRUARY 4

• FIFTH SUNDAY IN ORDINARY TIME •

My days are swifter than a weaver's shuttle;
they come to an end without hope.
Remember that my life is like the wind;
I shall not see happiness again.
—JOB 7:6–7

Are you ever like Job, feeling like you will never see happiness again? Remember that God heals the brokenhearted and binds up their wounds. As the poet Emily Dickinson writes, " 'Hope' is the thing with feathers that perches in the soul— / And sings the tune without the words— / And never stops—at all."

Job 7:1–4,6–7
Psalm 147:1–2,3–4,5–6
1 Corinthians 9:16–19,22–23
Mark 1:29–39

Monday

FEBRUARY 5

• ST. AGATHA, VIRGIN AND MARTYR •

*They scurried about the surrounding country and began to bring in the
sick on mats to wherever they heard he was.*
—MARK 6:55

When my husband, David, and I got married, we looked for
a church to attend where we both felt comfortable. I grew up
evangelical, he grew up Presbyterian, but we felt like we
needed a change—and a place for us to worship together as a
couple. The moment we stepped inside our church, Old
St. Pat's, in Chicago, we knew we had found our spiritual
home. The first year, we wept during every Mass. We were
each sick and hungry in our own way, and the words of the
liturgy, the grace we found there, the community—Jesus was
healing us. Wherever Jesus is found, we need to bring the
sick on their mats so they can be healed. Even if we are
those people.

1 Kings 8:1–7,9–13
Psalm 132:6–7,8–10
Mark 6:53–56

FEBRUARY 6

• ST. PAUL MIKI AND COMPANIONS, MARTYRS •

My soul yearns and pines
for the courts of the LORD.
My heart and my flesh
cry out for the living God.
—PSALM 84:3

My daughter yearns—pines—for the toy aisle at Target that
has American Girl-doll knockoffs. Many a shopping trip to
Target for toilet paper has been derailed by a meltdown in
the paper-goods section because she can't wait any longer to
visit her beloved doll aisle. And once she's there, it's
impossible to drag her away. When we love something that
much, we cry, plead, and wail to have it. Oh, how I wish that
my love for God were as passionate. How often do I pine and
yearn to go to Mass? And resist leaving once I'm there? What
can I do today to rekindle my love for God?

1 Kings 8:22–23,27–30
Psalm 84:3,4,5 and 10,11
Mark 7:1–13

"But what comes out of the man, that is what defiles him. From within the man, from his heart, come evil thoughts, unchastity, theft, murder, adultery, greed, malice, deceit, licentiousness, envy, blasphemy, arrogance, folly."
—MARK 7:20–22

Most religious traditions have rules. Growing up Baptist, we weren't allowed to dance or drink alcohol. Mormons shun caffeine. Catholics abstain from eating meat on Fridays. We all know people who observe every rule and tradition, but that's as deep as their faith goes. Throughout Scripture, Jesus spreads the message that he doesn't want us to just follow the rules, whatever they may be. It's not our habits that matter but the state of our hearts.

1 Kings 10:1–10
Psalm 37:30–31,39–40
Mark 7:14–23

FEBRUARY 8

• ST. JEROME EMILIANI, PRIEST * ST. JOSEPHINE BAKHITA, VIRGIN •

Blessed are they who observe what is right,
who do always what is just.
Remember us, O LORD, as you favor your people;
visit us with your saving help.
—PSALM 106:3–4

I have four siblings, and when we were young, my parents always made sure that we felt equally loved. They gave us the same number of presents at Christmas so no one would feel slighted. But it wasn't a perfect system. Inevitably, one of us would feel that another sibling was "Mom's favorite" or "Dad's favorite." Our country is founded on the ideal that everyone should be treated equally, but, as I so often felt growing up, we all know that's not how things are. We need to keep working to make things right, equal, and just, and to cry to God, "Visit us with your saving help!"

1 Kings 11:4–13
Psalm 106:3–4,35–36,37 and 40
Mark 7:24–30

FEBRUARY 9

"He has done all things well. He makes the deaf hear and the mute speak."
—MARK 7:37

People in the crowd begged Jesus to heal the deaf man. So Jesus took him away from the crowds and yelled to heaven, "Ephphatha!" which means "Be opened!" The man was immediately cured. This reminds me of videos I've seen online of deaf patients getting cochlear implants. You know the ones—where you see the patient's face suddenly light up, her eyes get big, and tears form because, suddenly, her world has opened up. She can hear! I recently saw a video of a baby, maybe six months old, who heard his mom's voice for the first time. First, he looked surprised, then confused, and then he started grinning and laughing. God, open our ears, our eyes, and our hearts so that we can be amazed, delighted, and filled with wonder.

1 Kings 11:29–32; 12:19
Psalm 81:10–11ab,12–13,14–15
Mark 7:31–37

Then, taking the seven loaves he gave thanks, broke them, and gave them to his disciples to distribute . . . They also had a few fish. He said the blessing over them and ordered them distributed also. They ate and were satisfied.

—MARK 8:6–7

Have you ever been so passionate about something that you skipped lunch? There were 4,000 people who were passionate enough to see Jesus even if it meant missing lunch and dinner. But Jesus had compassion. He took seven loaves and a few fishes, and somehow, that was enough for 4,000 people. This is what I love the most: "They were satisfied." So many parts of Scripture talk about our hunger, our thirst, our longing. God knows we have this desire to be fed, both physically and spiritually. And only he can satisfy.

1 Kings 12:26–32; 13:33–34
Psalm 106:6–7ab,19–20,21–22
Mark 8:1–10

Sunday

FEBRUARY 11

• SIXTH SUNDAY IN ORDINARY TIME •

A leper came to Jesus and kneeling down begged him and said, "If you wish, you can make me clean."
—MARK 1:40

In the Old Testament, someone who suffered from leprosy was considered unclean and was forced to rend his garments, shave his head, and live outside the camp. Leprosy is a cruel skin disease, and many sufferers lose toes, noses, and fingers as it progresses. It's contagious, so it's not surprising that lepers were forced to live outside the camp to avoid infecting others. But Jesus had pity on the leper and touched him. The leper was healed. We all have our own leprosy that Jesus wants to heal. St. Teresa of Calcutta, who ran a clinic for lepers in India, once called loneliness the "leprosy of the West." Whether it's loneliness or something else, what is your leprosy? Today, ask God to make you clean.

Leviticus 13:1–2,44–46
Psalm 32:1–2,5,11 (7)
1 Corinthians 10:31—11:1
Mark 1:40–45

FEBRUARY 12

Consider it all joy, my brothers and sisters, when you encounter various trials, for you know that the testing of your faith produces perseverance. And let perseverance be perfect, so that you may be perfect and complete, lacking in nothing.
—JAMES 1:2–4

After my mother died suddenly, I remember lying in bed, alone in my apartment (I was single at the time), and thinking, "I have never felt so alone in my life." I felt adrift in the middle of a dark ocean with no land in sight. Grief is a lonely journey. But now, years later, I see that time in my life as a crucible that made me humble and more compassionate and deepened my faith. I don't believe God causes our suffering, but as the poet Rumi writes, In the midst of ruin, treasures are found.

James 1:1–11
Psalm 119:67,68,71,72,75,76
Mark 8:11–13

FEBRUARY 13

Do you not yet understand or comprehend? Are your hearts hardened?
Do you have eyes and not see, ears and not hear?
—MARK 8:17–18

I'm convinced that when we go through times of doubt, it's
because we do not have the eyes to see the work God is
doing in our lives. God transforms us slowly, silently, subtly.
So slowly, silently, and subtly that sometimes we cannot see
it. We get impatient. We complain to God—*Where are you?*
We wonder if God is even there. But then something will
happen. It may not even be a big thing, but we will get a
glimpse of God. A signpost that assures us that God is
leading us home.

James 1:12–18
Psalm 94:12–13a,14–15,18–19
Mark 8:14–21

$\mathcal{W}ednesday$

FEBRUARY 14

Even now, says the LORD,
return to me with your whole heart,
with fasting, and weeping, and mourning;
Rend your hearts, not your garments,
and return to the LORD, your God.
—JOEL 2:12–13

The ancient Greek word *metanoia* means a transformative change of heart or changing one's mind. What turns us back to God? Maybe it's the sudden realization that our sin has left us anxious, tired, weary, and lonely. Maybe it's the grief that comes with knowing how much our sin has hurt other people or ourselves. Or maybe it's our lament that we have wasted time doing things that are empty and pointless. Whatever it is, there is a moment when we stop, turn around, and start walking toward God again. Jesus calls us to come back to him with our whole heart. Instead of being angry at us for drifting away, he offers us grace and mercy.

Joel 2:12–18
Psalm 51:3–4,5–6ab,12–13,14 and 17
2 Corinthians 5:20—6:2
Matthew 6:1–6,16–18

FEBRUARY 15

"For whoever wishes to save his life will lose it, but whoever loses his life for my sake will save it."
—LUKE 9:24

As I drove to the coffee shop to meet my now-husband, David, for the first time, I prayed, "God, help me love this person. I don't even know him, but please help me love him even if it's just for one date." In my years of dating, my focus had always been on me: *Will this person like me? What can he do for me?* In my selfishness, I had forgotten to ask, "How can I love this person?" Following Jesus means changing our focus from "What do I get out of this?" to "What am I willing to give up to become a more loving, compassionate follower of Christ?"

Deuteronomy 30:15–20
Psalm 1:1–2,3,4 and 6
Luke 9:22–25

FEBRUARY 16

This, rather, is the fasting that I wish:
releasing those bound unjustly,
untying the thongs of the yoke;
Setting free the oppressed,
breaking every yoke;
Sharing your bread with the hungry,
sheltering the oppressed and the homeless.
—ISAIAH 58:6–7

Throughout Scripture, Jesus condemns those who make a show out of their religiosity. He emphasizes that the Christian life is not about bowing down to idols, praying in public to impress people, or giving to the poor just to boost your reputation. In today's passage, Jesus condemns people who fast just for the sake of keeping a day of penance. Why not "fast" by doing something that's really going to matter, he says—like working for justice, sharing your bread with the hungry, or giving shelter to the homeless? Fasting and throwing a few coins into the cup of a homeless person isn't what it's all about.

Isaiah 58:1–9a
Psalm 51:3–4,5–6ab,18–19
Matthew 9:14–15

Then Levi gave a great banquet for him in his house, and a large crowd of tax collectors and others were at table with them.
—LUKE 5:29

Scripture is filled with banquets in which, most of the time, the rich and poor are eating together. Eating together presents a metaphor for the spiritual life. For, in breaking bread together, we acknowledge our need for nourishment but also our need for one another. Dorothy Day writes in *The Long Loneliness*, "The final word is love . . . to love we must know each other . . . and we know each other in the breaking of bread, and we are not alone any more. Heaven is a banquet and life is a banquet, too, even with a crust, where there is companionship. We have all known the long loneliness and we have learned that the only solution is love and that love comes with community."

Isaiah 58:9b–14
Psalm 86:1–2,3–4,5–6
Luke 5:27–32

Sunday

FEBRUARY 18

• FIRST SUNDAY OF LENT •

The Spirit drove Jesus out into the desert, and he remained in the desert
for forty days, tempted by Satan.
—MARK 1:12–13

The desert can be a desolate place, but maybe that desolation
offers an ideal setting for us to come face-to-face with
ourselves, deal with whatever we need to deal with, and hear
God's voice. One group of hermits, ascetics, and monks,
whom we now call the "Desert Fathers," found this to be true.
They were early Christians who lived in the Scetes desert of
Egypt in the third century. The wisdom that emerged from
these communities later influenced the Rule of St. Benedict,
inspired the model for Christian monasticism, and impacted
other movements like the Pietists. If you feel like you are in a
desert in your life, consider this wisdom from Abba Moses,
one of the Desert Fathers: "Sit in thy cell and thy cell will
teach thee all."

Genesis 9:8–15
Psalm 25:4–5,6–7,8–9
1 Peter 3:18–22
Mark 1:12–15

*"Amen, I say to you, whatever you did for one of these least
brothers of mine, you did for me."*
—MATTHEW 25:40

Congressman John Lewis fought his entire life for the least of
these. Lewis, a black man who was born to sharecroppers in
Alabama, played a crucial role in the Civil Rights movement
in the 1960s. He was one of the original thirteen Freedom
Riders, a group of black and white activists who rode buses
into the Deep South to challenge Southern states to uphold
the Supreme Court decision that declared segregated
interstate bus travel to be unconstitutional. He once said,
"Inside every human soul is the spark of the Divine." In
whom do you see the spark of the divine?

Leviticus 19:1–2,11–18
Psalm 19:8,9,10,15
Matthew 25:31–46

FEBRUARY 20

When the just cry out, the LORD hears them,
and from all their distress he rescues them.
The LORD is close to the brokenhearted;
and those who are crushed in spirit he saves.
—PSALM 34:18–19

We tend to want things to make sense, to be peaceful and comfortable. But more often than not, as soon as we start feeling comfortable—we're on top of our finances and careers, our families are doing well—something will disrupt that feeling. Maybe an illness, or a job loss, or a tragedy like 9/11. The question is, how do we remain steadfast amid the chaos? Know that Jesus is there, and he hears our cries and rescues us.

Isaiah 55:10–11
Psalm 34:4–5,6–7,16–17,18–19
Matthew 6:7–15

FEBRUARY 21

A clean heart create for me, O God,
and a steadfast spirit renew within me.
—PSALM 51:12

Healthy faith includes doubt. But sometimes, I long for an unwavering faith. In Charles Portis's novel *True Grit*, fourteen-year-old Mattie Ross is determined to find the man who murdered her father. She is unwavering in her quest, while everyone around her is astonished that a fourteen-year-old girl could have the courage and fortitude to seek justice. I want to have this same true grit in my faith in God. A steadfast spirit. Brave. Resolute.

Jonah 3:1–10
Psalm 51:3–4,12–13,18–19
Luke 11:29–32

FEBRUARY 22

• THE CHAIR OF ST. PETER, APOSTLE •

The LORD is my shepherd; I shall not want.
—PSALM 23:1

We live in a culture that is built on wanting more. We all feel a gnawing anxiety when we want what we don't have, a constant questioning of God's love and provision. But Scripture reminds us that if we follow Jesus, we can let go of our anxiety and constant striving for more. In him, we know that all shall be well. We can rest and be content.

1 Peter 5:1–4
Psalm 23:1–3a,4,5,6
Matthew 16:13–19

FEBRUARY 23

• ST. POLYCARP, BISHOP AND MARTYR •

You say, "The LORD's way is not fair!"
—EZEKIEL 18:25

God says that if a wicked man turns from his sins and does what is right and just, he shall surely live. But if a virtuous man turns from the path of virtue to do evil, he shall die.

This may seem unfair—do the virtuous man's previous actions not count? But it's all in the direction you're headed. If we want to have true life, we need to be walking toward God, not away from him.

Ezekiel 18:21–28
Psalm 130:1–2,3–4,5–7a,7bc–8
Matthew 5:20–26

FEBRUARY 24

*"But I say to you, love your enemies, and pray for those who
persecute you."*
—MATTHEW 5:44

I once had a boss who seemed to have a vendetta against me
for some unknown reason. I had recently gotten a
promotion, but when the department reorganized, he
became my new boss and started nitpicking everything I did.
I had to decide—what kind of person did I want to be? I
made an effort to be kind, to reach out to him, to try to have
compassion. We eventually became civil to each other, and
now, miraculously, we are friends. Most people don't really
understand why they do what they do. Christ said on the
cross, "Forgive them, for they know not what they do." Do
you have an enemy you need to forgive?

Deuteronomy 26:16–19
Psalm 119:1–2,4–5,7–8
Matthew 5:43–48

God put Abraham to the test. He called to him, "Abraham!" "Here I am!"
he replied.
—GENESIS 22:1

Abraham didn't hesitate. He said, "Here I am!" eagerly. When
God asked him to sacrifice his own son, he reached out and
took the knife. In this season of Lent, I am sacrificing eating
chocolate. But would I be willing to give up everything to
follow him? How much do I trust and love God?

Genesis 22:1–2,9a,10–13,15–18
Psalm 116:10,15,16–17,18–19
Romans 8:31b–34
Mark 9:2–10

FEBRUARY 26

Let the prisoners' sighing come before you;
with your great power free those doomed to death.
—PSALM 79:11

In 1997, Kelly Gissendaner plotted with her boyfriend to kill
her husband. For her crime, she was sentenced to death. It
was a horrible murder, but during her time in prison, she
found faith, ministered to other women in prison, and even
earned a theology degree from Emory University. It is a true
story of redemption, what the gospel is all about. Yet the
state of Georgia had no mercy. After several appeals,
clemency was denied. Even Pope Francis appealed to the
Georgia State Board of Pardons and Paroles to no avail. On
September 30, 2015, at 12:21 a.m., Gissendaner was put to
death by lethal injection. She sang "Amazing Grace" all the
way to the end. The state would not free her, but she was
truly free.

Daniel 9:4b–10
Psalm 79:8,9,11 and 13
Luke 6:36–38

"The scribes and the Pharisees have taken their seat on the chair of Moses. Therefore, do and observe all things whatsoever they tell you, but do not follow their example. For they preach but they do not practice. . . . All their works are performed to be seen."
—MATTHEW 23:2,3,5

I knew a pastor who was adored by his congregation. He was charming and good-looking and had a nice, well-heeled family. But then I learned that this pastor had been having an affair. We hear stories like this time and time again. Leaders fail us. They do not practice what they preach. Jesus tells the crowd that we have one master: Christ. And "whoever exalts himself will be humbled; but whoever humbles himself will be exalted." (Matthew 23:12) Don't be fooled by leaders who just want the spotlight. Live humbly. Serve God quietly.

Isaiah 1:10,16–20
Psalm 50:8–9,16bc–17,21 and 23
Matthew 23:1–12

But my trust is in you, O LORD;
I say, "You are my God."
In your hands is my destiny.
—PSALM 31:15–16

When something goes wrong, I often spiral down into a pit of despair, thinking the world is going to end. Our new car is dripping oil, and I think we'll have to pay thousands of dollars to get it fixed. Turns out the oil cap wasn't tight enough. I see my bosses together in a conference room, and I imagine that must mean the company isn't doing well. Turns out they were just discussing the company holiday party. My husband and I have a fight, and I worry that we are headed for divorce. But then the next day we forgive each other. I want to be like the psalmist and say: *My destiny is in your hands, God. Help me rest in you.*

Jeremiah 18:18–20
Psalm 31:5–6,14,15–16
Matthew 20:17–28

Thursday

MARCH 1

Blessed is the man who trusts in the LORD,
whose hope is the LORD.
He is like a tree planted beside the waters
that stretches out its roots to the stream.
—JEREMIAH 17:7–8

Our neighborhood is filled with 100-year-old trees that line
our street like sentries. But in the past few years, many of
those trees have been toppled by 70-mile-an-hour winds that
often accompany summer storms. The trees are like fallen
soldiers, and I mourn the loss. Most of the trees were planted
between the sidewalk and the street, their roots probably
entangled with cement, sewer pipes, and
basements—impediments that make the roots weak. We
often can't see what goes on below the surface, but it's of
utmost importance. As our trust and hope grow deeper and
deeper, the roots of our faith stretch to the cool waters that
quench our thirst and keep us strong.

Jeremiah 17:5–10
Psalm 1:1–2,3,4 and 6
Luke 16:19–31

"Here comes that master dreamer! Come on, let us kill him and throw him into one of the cisterns here; we could say that a wild beast devoured him. We shall then see what comes of his dreams."
—GENESIS 37:19–20

Joseph's brothers were burning with envy because Joseph was the favored son and a dreamer. Because of their envy, his brothers decided to kill their own flesh and blood. I can see myself in the brothers—envious of those around me who are living out their dreams. In my first confession as a Catholic, I confessed my envy. The priest asked me, "What do you really want?" I said, "I want to know that God loves me." At the root of my envy, I want to know that I am God's beloved child and that he wants good things for me. What is at the root of your envy?

Genesis 37:3–4,12–13a,17b–28a
Psalm 105:16–17,18–19,20–21
Matthew 21:33–43,45–46

"Father, I have sinned against heaven and against you. I no longer deserve to be called your son; treat me as you would treat one of your hired workers."
—LUKE 15:18–19

Today's Gospel reading is the well-known parable of the prodigal son, who takes his father's inheritance and squanders it and then returns to his father's estate asking to be treated like one of the servants. Instead, his father has a party and kills the fatted calf. I admit I often feel like the prodigal son—so undeserving. But sometimes I am also like the brother, who complains that his father has never thrown him a party. His father tells him, "My son, you are here with me always; everything I have is yours." Which son are you today? The one who feels undeserving and ashamed? Or the one who is overlooking what God has already given him?

Micah 7:14–15,18–20
Psalm 103:1–2,3–4,9–10,11–12
Luke 15:1–3,11–32

Sunday

MARCH 4

• THIRD SUNDAY OF LENT •

You shall not covet your neighbor's house.
—EXODUS 20:17

I admit it: I covet houses. I look at houses online, imagining what it would be like to live in the ones I like. Realtor.com, Zillow.com, and RedFin.com are my weaknesses. Maybe it's because both of my parents were Realtors, but when I drive through neighborhoods, I try to estimate how much each house costs and wonder if we could ever afford one. I live on the North Side of Chicago, where it boggles my mind how many old, beautiful mansions there are, some even with private beaches on Lake Michigan. How do people make enough money to afford one? It is beyond me. To covet is to have "an inordinate or wrongful desire," according to the dictionary. God, forgive me my wrongful desire and help me be content with what you have given me, which is abundant. Amen.

Exodus 20:1–17 or 20:1–3,7–8,12–17
Psalm 19:8,9,10,11
1 Corinthians 1:22–25
John 2:13–25

Send forth your light and your fidelity;
they shall lead me on
And bring me to your holy mountain,
to your dwelling-place.
—PSALM 43:3

One summer, we went to a campground in Michigan. As city folks, we weren't used to the dark, and light pollution prevents us from seeing the stars. At the campground, another family invited us to a campfire. I stepped out of our cabin and breathed in the darkness as I saw a shooting star. David had a flashlight, but it was dark along the path. Desta was scared. "Mommy, what if there are animals?!" I assured her we didn't have far to go, and Daddy's light would show us the way. Soon we spotted the fire and breathed a sigh of relief. We often wait for God to show us our destination. Instead, we can only see enough to take the next step. That is enough.

2 Kings 5:1–15b
Psalm 42:2,3; 43:3,4
Luke 4:24–30

*"Lord, if my brother sins against me, how often must I forgive him?
As many as seven times?" Jesus answered, "I say to you, not seven times
but seventy-seven times."*
—MATTHEW 18:21–22

My daughter collects rocks. Just ordinary rocks that she puts into a small suitcase my sister gave her, which now weighs about ten pounds. "No," I tell her. "You cannot bring your rock collection with you on vacation." I collect grudges like Desta collects rocks. I mull over wrongs done to me. Rehash conversations. Passive-aggressively "snub" people for some minor offense. It's ugly and dark and isolating. After a while, these grudges get too heavy. Jesus calls me to forgive. Not just forgive once, but over and over and over again, to let the rocks fall out of my suitcase. One by one, I drop them behind me on the path, and I walk faster because my load is light.

Daniel 3:25,34–43
Psalm 25:4–5ab,6 and 7bc,8 and 9
Matthew 18:21–35

Wednesday

MARCH 7

• SS. PERPETUA AND FELICITY, MARTYRS •

"However, take care and be earnestly on your guard not to forget the things which your own eyes have seen, nor let them slip from your memory as long as you live, but teach them to your children and to your children's children."
—DEUTERONOMY 4:9

"All shall be well, and all shall be well, and all manner of things shall be well," said Julian of Norwich. The older I get, the more I know this to be true. I have collected memories of God's goodness like seashells on the beach and stored them away in a jar in my soul. I know that even when the worst things happen, it's an opportunity for redemption and resurrection. My seven-year-old daughter doesn't have those memories yet, and she needs me to tell her. The other day she was afraid of what would happen to her if David and I died. I held her and tried to calm her fears. You will be okay, I told her. You will collect seashells yourself throughout your life, but you can borrow some of mine, now. I'm here to tell you that all shall be well.

Deuteronomy 4:1,5–9
Psalm 147:12–13,15–16,19–20
Matthew 5:17–19

Thursday

MARCH 8

• ST. JOHN OF GOD, RELIGIOUS •

This is what I commanded my people: Listen to my voice; then I will be your God and you shall be my people.
—JEREMIAH 7:23

In marriage counseling, some couples practice "Imago dialogue," where one person talks and then the other person repeats back what was said to make sure that he or she understands. Communicating in this way helps each person feel truly, deeply understood. It's the same thing with listening to God. Many of us may find it difficult to hear God's voice. We go about our day, thinking about our own agenda, not really paying attention. But if we want to be in relationship with God, we need to listen to him. As French philosopher Simone Weil said, "Attention is the rarest and purest form of generosity." How are you paying attention to God today?

Jeremiah 7:23–28
Psalm 95:1–2,6–7,8–9
Luke 11:14–23

"You shall love your neighbor as yourself."
—MARK 12:31

I bought my condo right before the Great Recession. You can probably guess what happened. A few years after I moved in, the value plunged to about half of what I bought it for. In the meantime, I got married and adopted a child; we outgrew the place years ago. But something interesting has happened during these years. Our neighbors have stayed as well, and we have become good friends with many of them. We decided to love those around us, and the result is that our condo building has turned into a wonderful little community. Now the values are back up to almost what they were, and we are finally getting ready to move. But now I hate the thought of moving and leaving the neighbors whom we love.

Hosea 14:2–10
Psalm 81:6c–8a,8bc–9,10–11ab,14 and 17
Mark 12:28–34

MARCH 10

"O God, I thank you that I am not like the rest of humanity—greedy, dishonest, adulterous—or even like this tax collector. I fast twice a week, and I pay tithes on my whole income."
—LUKE 18:11–12

I always thought that God would "bless" me if I did everything right. I followed all the rules. I was like the Pharisee in this passage, listing off all the things that made me superior to everyone else. But in this Scripture reading, it's the tax collector who hangs his head in shame and prays "O God, be merciful to me a sinner" who is justified. Jesus said it's the humble who will be exalted. God doesn't want our rule-keeping and arrogance. He wants us to recognize our need for mercy. Whom are you like today, the Pharisee or the tax collector?

Hosea 6:1–6
Psalm 51:3–4,18–19,20–21ab
Luke 18:9–14

"But whoever lives the truth comes to the light, so that his works may be clearly seen as done in God."
—JOHN 3:21

Just like Adam and Eve in the garden, we hide when we are ashamed. We eat too much and hide the candy wrappers at the bottom of the garbage so that our family can't see. We surf the Internet and then clear our cache so no one knows how much time we wasted or what websites we visited. We tell our boss that the report is "almost done" when, in reality, we haven't even started. How freeing it is to live in the light and be seen clearly by God. To live in a way that makes us proud of our actions. We don't have to hide anymore.

2 Chronicles 36:14–16,19–23
Psalm 137:1–2,3,4–5,6 (6ab)
Ephesians 2:4–10
John 3:14–21

MARCH 12

Thus says the LORD:
Lo, I am about to create new heavens
and a new earth; . . .
No longer shall the sound of weeping be heard there,
or the sound of crying.
—ISAIAH 65:17,19

I recently found out that my brother-in-law has a mass on his lung. We don't know what it is yet, but when a doctor says "mass on your lung," there is fear. And tears. As I talked to my sister last night, she cried off and on throughout our phone conversation. In Psalm 13, the psalmist writes, "How long, LORD?" How long will we have to live in this world where there is so much sickness, sadness, and grief? I find hope in this Scripture that reminds us that in the new heavens and new earth that God is creating, there will be no weeping. Come, Lord Jesus.

Isaiah 65:17–21
Psalm 30:2 and 4,5–6,11–12a and 13b
John 4:43–54

MARCH 13

"Wherever the river flows, every sort of living creature that can multiple shall live."
—EZEKIEL 47:9

I live about a mile from Lake Michigan, and when the weather is nice I jog to the lake and sit on the pier. I walk along the beach and look for sea glass. I breathe in the fresh air and watch the waves. It restores my weary soul. The man in today's Gospel reading longs to get to the pool to be healed, but he can't walk, so someone always beats him to it. Jesus heals him on the spot. In Scripture, Jesus refers to himself as "living water." Many of us may find that going to the beach or lake can restore our souls for a time. But we also long for the living water that will heal us completely.

Ezekiel 47:1–9,12
Psalm 46:2–3,5–6,8–9
John 5:1–16

MARCH 14

But Zion said, "The LORD has forsaken me;
my Lord has forgotten me.
Can a mother forget her infant,
be without tenderness for the child of her womb?
Even should she forget,
I will never forget you."
—ISAIAH 49:14–15

Have you ever felt that God has forgotten about you? Maybe you're single and wanting to be married, or maybe you're married and longing for a child, or maybe you're unemployed and looking for a job. "When is God going to show up?!" you may ask yourself. You can find comfort in the fact that followers of Christ have been asking that question for centuries, and his answer is always: I will never forget you. Rest in that today.

Isaiah 49:8–15
Psalm 145:8–9,13cd–14,17–18
John 5:17–30

Thursday

MARCH 15

"Go down at once to your people whom you brought out of the land of Egypt, for they have become depraved. They have soon turned aside from the way I pointed out to them, making for themselves a molten calf and worshiping it."
—EXODUS 32:7–8

When we forget what God has done, we start worshipping idols. When we forget that time God helped us out of a financial mess and think it's all up to us to make enough money to fix it ourselves, we are worshipping money. When we forget how beloved we are and think we need to be perfect to be loved, we are worshipping the approval of others. You get the idea. "Do this in remembrance of me," Christ said at the Last Supper. Maybe Christ knew that we would struggle to remember and instead bow down to the molten calf.

Exodus 32:7–14
Psalm 106:19–20,21–22,23
John 5:31–47

⇒ 103 ⇐

Friday

MARCH 16

So they tried to arrest him, but no one laid a hand upon him, because his hour had not yet come.
—JOHN 7:30

Jesus had a mission to fulfill, but his hour had not yet come. We may often lament the time we have wasted, the opportunities we have missed. But God is bigger than our regrets. Do you feel like you missed your chance? Don't worry. God will work through you in his time.

Wisdom 2:1a,12–22
Psalm 34:17–18,19–20,21 and 23
John 7:1–2,10,25–30

"The Christ will not come from Galilee, will he?"
—JOHN 7:41

I moved back home after college to attend graduate school, and immediately fell into a deep depression. I had become a different person, but my parents still treated me like the eighteen-year-old who had left home four years earlier. They did not recognize who I had become. When Jesus returns to Galilee, his former neighbors and friends do not recognize him. People are confused over whether he is Christ. How often do we not recognize Christ in our midst because he looks so different than what we had thought?

Jeremiah 11:18–20
Psalm 7:2–3,9bc–10,11–12
John 7:40–53

In the days when Christ Jesus was in the flesh, he offered prayers and supplications with loud cries and tears to the one who was able to save him from death.

—HEBREWS 5:7

Every once in a while in Scripture, we get a glimpse of Christ's humanity. Today's passage reads, "When Christ Jesus was in the flesh," he prayed and cried out to God. There's something so comforting about this. Jesus understands our tears. He knows our cries. He has been there too.

Jeremiah 31:31–34
Psalm 51:3–4,12–13,14–15
Hebrews 5:7–9
John 12:20–33

"Why were you looking for me? Did you not know that I must be in my Father's house?"
—LUKE 2:49

In today's reading, Jesus is twelve years old and has stayed behind in Jerusalem, unbeknownst to his parents, who are traveling back to Nazareth. Like any parents, they panic and go to look for him. He was sitting among teachers in the temple. "Why were you looking for me?" he asks. He sounds sure of himself—almost annoyed that they don't understand his need to fulfill his mission. I wonder if this is the point when Mary and Joseph realize their son's divinity.

2 Samuel 7:4–5a,12–14a,16
Psalm 89:2–3,4–5,27 and 29
Romans 4:13,16–18,22
Matthew 1:16,18–21,24a or Luke 2:41–51a

He said to them, "You belong to what is below, I belong to what is above."
—JOHN 8:23

The Pharisees could not see beyond their own rules and judgments, their black-and-white world where everything is either right or wrong. They were trapped in their own piousness. They had no vision for the freedom that could be found in Christ's kingdom. In his poem "Coming into the Kingdom," Christian Wiman writes of this freedom—of what is above: "Coming into the kingdom I was like a man stealing into freedom when the tyrant dies. . . . I came into the damp and dirtlight of late November in north Chicago, where . . . wires cross the alley like a random run, and an airplane splits and sutures the blue as it roars for elsewhere."

Numbers 21:4–9
Psalm 102:2–3,16–18,19–21
John 8:21–30

"Amen, Amen I say to you, everyone who commits sin is a slave of sin."
—JOHN 8:34

I love the scene in the movie *The Shawshank Redemption* when
the main character, Andy Dufresne, after crawling through
the sewage pipes of the prison, finally reaches the outside
world and raises his hands toward heaven, rejoicing. We are
often like Andy, crawling through the sewer pipes of our own
sins of envy, greed, gluttony, self-absorption, arrogance,
indifference, pride, and lust. Sin is its own punishment. If we
envy someone, eventually that envy will cripple us and
damage relationships. If we are gluttonous, gradually our
gluttony will damage our bodies and souls. If we are
self-absorbed, our absorption will make us feel lonely. And so
on. Jesus came to save us from ourselves. Scripture says, if the
"Son frees you, then you will truly be free." What sin do you
need to be freed from today?

Daniel 3:14–20,91–92,95
Daniel 3:52,53,54,55,56
John 8:31–42

"I will render you exceedingly fertile; I will make nations of you; kings shall stem from you."
—GENESIS 17:6

Research suggests that psychological trauma can be passed on to a person's children through unconscious cues or affective messages that flow between child and adult, and may even be passed through our DNA. As a parent, I'm very aware of what I'm passing along to my daughter. She picks up on everything—my response to anger, my anxiety, my mannerisms. We do not know the power we have to influence those coming behind us. God works through individuals but also through generations. The seeds of my faith, although it looks different than my parents', was born from what they passed along to me. What am I passing on to Desta? And what are you passing on to the next generation?

Genesis 17:3–9
Psalm 105:4–5,6–7,8–9
John 8:51–59

*"Sing to the LORD,
praise the LORD,
For he has rescued the life of the poor
from the power of the wicked!"*
—JEREMIAH 20:13

I live in Chicago, where I encounter poverty every day.
Homeless people beg for money at intersections, carrying
their paper cups up and down the rows of cars stopped at
stoplights. I regularly visit friends and my daughter's
extended birth family in neighborhoods where children don't
have a chance because money for public schools has been
siphoned off by corrupt politicians, leaving the schools with
few resources. It's unfair and unjust, and it's easy to fall into
despair. Today's Scripture reminds me that God is just, he
will rescue the poor, and our hope is in him.

Jeremiah 20:10–13
Psalm 18:2–3a,3bc–4,5–6,7
John 10:31–42

MARCH 24

*Many of the Jews who had come to Mary and seen what Jesus had done
began to believe in him. But some of them went to the Pharisees and told
them what Jesus had done.*
—JOHN 11:45–46

We have a choice: to see what God is doing in the world and
participate in that grace or to be a skeptic and run away in
fear or disbelief. God is working in us and in the world. It's
up to us to keep our eyes open to seeing it. Otherwise, we'll
run away afraid and alarmed and hunker down into our safe
bunkers. In this reading, the Pharisees were so threatened by
Jesus that they planned to kill him. That's what fear does to
people. And that's probably why, throughout Scripture, Jesus
says, "Do not be afraid."

Ezekiel 37:21–28
Jeremiah 31:10,11–12abcd,13
John 11:45–56

MARCH 25

• PALM SUNDAY OF THE PASSION OF THE LORD •

"Abba, Father, all things are possible to you. Take this cup away from me, but not what I will but what you will."

—MARK 14:36

For most of my life, I experienced Christ's passion from a distance, observing Christ's life, death, and resurrection from the sidelines. But then a spiritual mentor taught me that as Christians, we participate in the paschal mystery—the process of living, dying, being resurrected—throughout our lives.

With every loss comes new life in some form. When my mother died suddenly when I was thirty-six, I couldn't imagine a more earth-shattering loss. *Take this cup from me,* I begged God. *Don't let this be true.* And yet, in the months following her death, in my deepest grief I experienced the deepest joy. God showed his grace in the most poignant ways. How have you experienced resurrection in loss?

PROCESSION:
Mark 11:1–10 or John 12:12–16

MASS:
Isaiah 50:4–7
Psalm 22:8–9,17–18,19–20,23–24
Philippians 2:6–11
Mark 14:1—15:47 or 15:1–39

Monday

MARCH 26

• MONDAY OF HOLY WEEK •

*I formed you, and set you
as a covenant of the people,
a light for the nations,
To open the eyes of the blind,
to bring out prisoners from confinement,
and from the dungeon, those who live in darkness.*
—Isaiah 42:6–7

Prisons can take many forms. We can be confined by our own depression, our own jealousies, or our own unmet desires. Our minds churn with thoughts of wanting life to be different, to be easier, to be better. We are blind to how God is working in us, through us, and beside us. On this Monday of Holy Week, we have the hope that Jesus will bring us out of the dungeons of our own making. He will bring us out of this darkness into light.

Isaiah 42:1–7
Psalm 27:1,2,3,13–14
John 12:1–11

*"Where I am going, you cannot follow me now, though you will
follow later."*
—JOHN 13:36

The disciples are trying to make sense of what Jesus is saying
to them—and of what is going to happen. He is going to
leave, but they cannot follow. At least not now. Jesus is going
to lay down his life for them. Later, Peter says, "Master, why
can I not follow you now? I will lay down my life for you."
And Jesus answers, "Will you lay down your life for me?" I see
this now as central to the paschal mystery. Jesus laid down
his life for us, and he asks us if we are willing to follow his
example. Will you lay down your life for Christ? What are
you willing to give up to follow him?

Isaiah 49:1–6
Psalm 71:1–2,3–4a,5ab–6ab,15 and 17
John 13:21–33,36–38

"For the LORD hears the poor,
and his own who are in bonds he spurns not."
—PSALM 69:33

The poor will always be with us, says Jesus. Some of my
daughter's birth family struggle to make enough money to
live. They are at a disadvantage in our society, never having
had the foundation of resources, good education, or mentors
to help them navigate life. So many times the poor are
blamed for their own lot in life. "Pull yourselves up by your
bootstraps!" some tell them. But so many have so much
further to pull themselves up, it's almost impossible. And yet
Christ does not blame them. He hears their cries. If Christ's
Passion isn't about offering hope to even the most destitute,
then what is it about?

Isaiah 50:4–9a
Psalm 69:8–10,21–22,31 and 33–34
Matthew 26:14–25

Thursday

MARCH 29

"Today this Scripture passage is fulfilled in your hearing."
—LUKE 4:21

Jesus went to the synagogue in Nazareth, his hometown, and read what the prophet Isaiah proclaimed: "The Spirit of the Lord is upon me, / because he has anointed me / to bring glad tidings to the poor. / He has sent me to proclaim liberty to captives / and recovery of sight to the blind, / to let the oppressed go free, / and to proclaim a year acceptable to the Lord." The crowd looked intently at Jesus and he said, I am the fulfillment of this prophecy. It's me. I'm here. I will set the captives free, make the blind see, give the poor hope. Today, as we anticipate Good Friday and Easter, let's praise God that this prophecy has been fulfilled.

CHRISM MASS:
Isaiah 61:1–3a,6a,8b–9
Psalm 89:21–22,25 and 27
Revelation 1:5–8
Luke 4:16–21

EVENING MASS OF THE
LORD'S SUPPER:
Exodus 12:1–8,11–14
Psalm 116:12–13,15–16bc,17–18
1 Corinthians 11:23–26
John 13:1–15

"It is finished."
—JOHN 19:30

My first Good Friday service as a Catholic, I watched worshippers line up to venerate the cross. I saw young and old, rich and poor, black and white, people from all walks of life carrying who-knows-what kind of sorrows and burdens, make their way down the marble aisle, kneel, and gently kiss the rough wood that symbolized Christ's suffering. It reminded me of the end of Flannery O'Connor's short story "Revelation," when the main character, Mrs. Turpin, sees a vision of a "vast swinging bridge extending upward from the earth through a field of living fire. Upon it a vast horde of souls were rumbling toward heaven." Today, as we meditate on Jesus' death with a vast horde of souls, let us remember, dying is not the end. As pastor and author Tony Campolo says: "It's Friday, but Sunday's coming!"

Isaiah 52:13—53:12
Psalm 31:2,6,12–13,15–16,17,25
Hebrews 4:14–16; 5:7–9
John 18:1—19:42

Saturday

MARCH 31

• HOLY SATURDAY •

I shall not die, but live,
and declare the works of the LORD.
—PSALM 118:17

Now, we wait for his Resurrection and our own resurrection.
This is the liminal time when that old life you were living is
dead. Maybe it's because you lost your marriage or your job,
or someone close to you died. It's a wilderness, really, when
the old "you" is dead, but it's not clear yet what your new,
resurrected life will be like. This waiting is hard. We don't
like not knowing. But on Easter Vigil, watch for the light.
The light will come and fill the entire sanctuary. For just as
we celebrate Christ's Resurrection tomorrow, we will also
soon celebrate our own.

EASTER VIGIL:
Genesis 1:1—2:2 or 1:1,26–31a
Psalm 104:1–2,5–6,10,12,13–14,24,35 or
33:4–5,6–7,12–13,20–22 (5b)
Genesis 22:1–18 or 22:1–2,9a,10–13,15–18
Psalm 16:5,8,9–10,11 (1)
Exodus 14:15—15:1
Exodus 15:1–2,3–4,5–6,17–18
Isaiah 54:5–14
Psalm 30:2,4,5–6,11–12,13
Isaiah 55:1–11

Isaiah 12:2–3,4,5–6
Baruch 3:9–15,32—4:4
Psalm 19:8,9,10,11
Ezekiel 36:16–17a,18–28
Psalm 42:3,5; 43:3,4 or
Isaiah 12:2–3,4bcd,5–6 or
Psalm 51:12–13,14–15,18–19
Romans 6:3–11
Psalm 118:1–2,16–17,22–23
Mark 16:1–7

⇒ 119 ⇐

Sunday

APRIL 1

• EASTER SUNDAY OF THE RESURRECTION OF THE LORD •

*For they did not yet understand the Scripture that he had to rise
from the dead.*
—JOHN 20:9

I have three sisters, and when we were young, my mother
sewed us Easter dresses, which we wore with white knee
socks and shiny Mary Jane shoes to the sunrise service at our
little Baptist church a mile up the hill from where we lived.
Along with my little brother, dressed in a baby-blue
seersucker suit, we watched the sun rise from the hill, sang
"Christ the Lord Is Risen Today," prayed, and then ate
cinnamon rolls in the church basement. Later, after the main
Easter service, we went home and found our Easter baskets
amongst the blooming spring flowers in our yard. These
memories are filled with light and sun and goodness. But I
did not yet understand what it all meant, that Christ's
Resurrection was everything—our salvation and our hope.

Acts 10:34a,37–43
Psalm 118:1–2,16–17,22–23
Colossians 3:1–4 or 1 Corinthians 5:6b–8
John 20:1–9 or Mark 16:1–7 or (at an
afternoon or evening Mass) Luke 24:13–35

They approached, embraced his feet, and did him homage. Then Jesus said to them, "Do not be afraid."
—MATTHEW 28:9–10

Mary Magdalene and the other Mary saw that the tomb was empty, and they were filled with joy, but they were also fearful. They ran to tell the disciples, and on their way, they met Jesus. The first thing Jesus said to them was "Do not be afraid." I wonder if they had really thought, before his Resurrection, that all was lost. That the miracles, the sermons, the followers, were all for naught. That they had all been fools to follow him. But then, when they saw him standing there in the road, there must have been joy but also surprise at this power that had made him live again. God's power can be awesome, but we must first get past our fears to see him.

Acts 2:14,22–33
Psalm 16:1–2a and 5,7–8,9–10,11
Matthew 28:8–15

Tuesday

APRIL 3

• TUESDAY WITHIN THE OCTAVE OF EASTER •

"Let the whole house of Israel know for certain that God has made him both Lord and Christ, this Jesus whom you crucified."
—ACTS 2:36

It's possible to believe in Jesus as the Christ and not make him your Lord. What is the difference? The word *Christ* is a Greek word that is the equivalent of "Messiah" in Hebrew. Christ is the fulfillment of Isaiah's prophecy. But *Lord* is another thing entirely. When you proclaim Jesus as Lord, you are willing to submit to his will. So many times I talk about Christ, but am I really making him Lord of my life? Am I surrendering to what he is doing in and through me? It is only when we surrender our lives to Jesus that he can save us and make us whole.

Acts 2:36–41
Psalm 33:4–5,18–19,20 and 22
John 20:11–18

Wednesday

APRIL 4

• WEDNESDAY WITHIN THE OCTAVE OF EASTER •

And it happened that, while he was with them at table, he took bread,
said the blessing, broke it, and gave it to them. With that their eyes were
opened and they recognized him.
—LUKE 24:30–31

I've always found it surprising that the two disciples who
encountered Jesus after his Resurrection did not recognize
him. How could they not know it was him? Maybe because
they weren't expecting to see him. They thought the whole
thing was over—that Christ was supposed to be dead. It's
kind of like when you see a friend out of context and don't
immediately recognize him or her. Once, my old youth
pastor (whom I hadn't seen in fifteen years) showed up in my
workplace because my company had hired him as a
consultant. It took me a few minutes to realize who he was. If
the disciples couldn't even recognize Jesus, is it any wonder
that we sometimes don't recognize him in our lives?

Acts 3:1–10
Psalm 105:1–2,3–4,6–7,8–9
Luke 24:13–35

Thursday

APRIL 5

"Why are you troubled? And why do questions arise in your hearts?
Look at my hands and my feet, that it is I myself. Touch me and see,
because a ghost does not have flesh and bones as you can see I have."
—LUKE 24:38–39

The risen Christ appeared once again to the disciples, and
they still had a hard time believing it was him. So Jesus said,
"Touch me and see." One thing I love about being Catholic is
how tangible and physical it is. During Mass, we stand, we
kneel, we make the sign of the cross, we feel the bread and
wine on our tongues. We dip our fingers into water and cross
ourselves to remember our baptisms. All these things are
reminders that Christ is real and in our midst.

Acts 3:11–26
Psalm 8:2ab and 5,6–7,8–9
Luke 24:35–48

When it was already dawn, Jesus was standing on the shore; but the
disciples did not realize that it was Jesus.
—JOHN 21:4

Christ appears to the disciples for the third time. And once
more, they do not recognize him. (You'd think they would
by now.) This time, they are fishing, and Jesus is on the
shore. He tells them to cast their nets, and low and behold
they catch so many fish that they have trouble bringing in
the nets. "It is the Lord," Peter says. They jump out of the
boat and run to Jesus, who tells them, "Come, have
breakfast." He builds a fire, breaks bread for them, cooks the
fish. I love this scene: the resurrected Jesus cooking a
campfire breakfast for the disciples after a long night of
fishing. A beautiful picture of how he fills us, comforts us,
and gives us what we need.

Acts 4:1–12
Psalm 118:1–2 and 4,22–24,25–27a
John 21:1–14

"It is impossible for us not to speak about what we have seen and heard."
—ACTS 4:20

The leaders, elders, and scribes recognized Peter and John as companions of Jesus—and saw them as uneducated and ordinary. They warned Peter and John not to speak or teach at all in the name of Jesus. Peter and John, however, defied the leaders. How could they not talk about Christ after everything they had seen? When we are changed by what Jesus has done in our lives, we cannot keep silent.

Acts 4:13–21
Psalm 118:1 and 14–15ab,16–18,19–21
Mark 16:9–15

Sunday

APRIL 8

• SECOND SUNDAY OF EASTER • SUNDAY OF DIVINE MERCY •

The community of believers was of one heart and mind, and no one claimed that any of his possessions was his own, but they had everything in common.
—ACTS 4:32

In the book *The Gift*, author Lewis Hyde writes about how when the Puritans first arrived in America, they discovered that Native Americans had an odd view of possessions. They would offer someone a gift, say a pipe carved from stone. That person would take the gift home and keep it. But soon, another friend would visit and expect the host to give him the pipe as a gift. The Native Americans viewed "gifts" as objects that would continually be given to others, constantly circulating throughout the tribe. While the phrase "Indian giver" has a bad connotation, Native Americans actually had a very generous and communal view of their possessions. What a beautiful picture of how the body of Christ should work.

Acts 4:32–35
Psalm 118:2–4,13–15,22–24
1 John 5:1–6
John 20:19–31

"May it be done to me according to your word."
—LUKE 1:38

Growing up evangelical, I didn't think much about Mary. But since becoming Catholic, I have tried to understand her. Does she, as some think, disempower women because she represents passive submission? Or can she provide a different kind of strength, a model for how we can live out our faith? In an NPR interview, writer Caroline Langston discussed how Mary can represent the latter: "Millions of people in this country practice yoga to acquire inner calm or look to Buddhism or Sufism for the tools of contemplation or join 12-step programs to admit they are powerless, but they should not lose sight of the fact that an image of peace and stillness is inherent in Christianity, too, in Mary, the mother of God, pregnant with life and wonder, who teaches us to be rapt observers before the incomprehensible mysteries of existence."

Isaiah 7:10–14; 8:10
Psalm 40:7–8a,8b–9,10,11
Hebrews 10:4–10
Luke 1:26–38

APRIL 10

There was no needy person among them.
—ACTS 4:34

The early followers of Christ had a unity that we should all strive for. Can you imagine what it would be like to have a place where people shared what they had so that no one would go hungry or homeless? What can we do in our own communities that would make us more like the early Christians? Is there something you have that you could give to someone who needs it more? Is there a needy person in your community with whom you can share your gifts and talents or presence?

Acts 4:32–37
Psalm 93:1ab,1cd–2,5
John 3:7b–15

APRIL 11

• ST. STANISLAUS, BISHOP AND MARTYR •

For God did not send his Son into the world to condemn the world, but
that the world might be saved through him.
—JOHN 3:17

Religious people throughout the ages have confused
following the rules with being saved. The Pharisees kept all
the laws and condemned everyone else who didn't keep
them, including Jesus. But when Jesus entered the picture, he
challenged the Pharisees' worldview. He showed us that God
isn't a cosmic attorney who relates to us in a court of law.
Instead, he wants to be our lover. He wants our hearts.

Acts 5:17–26
Psalm 34:2–3,4–5,6–7,8–9
John 3:16–21

Thursday

APRIL 12

The LORD is close to the brokenhearted,
and those who are crushed in spirit he saves.
—PSALM 34:19

When I lost my mother suddenly, I had no idea how lonely grief could be. Grief is isolating, because we all grieve in our own way. Our grief can make us more compassionate toward others who grieve, and yet no one can fully enter another's grief. But this psalm reminds us that the Lord is close to those who are brokenhearted. Nicholas Wolterstorff, who lost his twenty-five-year-old son in a mountain climbing accident, wrote a classic book on grief called *Lament for a Son*. In it, he writes, "We strain to hear. But instead of hearing an answer we catch sight of God himself scraped and torn. Through our tears we see the tears of God." Whatever you are grieving today, be comforted that God knows your grief—and he is crying too.

Acts 5:27–33
Psalm 34:2 and 9,17–18,19–20
John 3:31–36

Friday

APRIL 13

• ST. MARTIN I, POPE AND MARTYR •

Wait for the LORD with courage;
be stouthearted, and wait for the LORD.
—PSALM 27:14

Stouthearted means being resolute, brave, audacious, bold, gutsy. It was often used to describe knights. I don't act much like a knight when I'm waiting for God. I'm whiny, impatient, and pitiful. Not a pretty picture. But I love the image of a knight standing at attention, bravely waiting for his next orders. God, give me a stout heart so I can stand gallantly, courageously, and patiently as I wait for you.

Acts 5:34–42
Psalm 27:1,4,13–14
John 6:1–15

Saturday
APRIL 14

When they had rowed about three or four miles, they saw Jesus walking on the sea and coming near the boat, and they began to be afraid. But he said to them, "It is I. Do not be afraid."
—JOHN 6:19–20

When my husband and I had the opportunity to adopt our daughter through foster care, I was terrified. I was afraid of becoming a mother, of losing my independence and freedom, and of dealing with the foster care system. But I overcame my fear and said yes. It has been the best decision I've ever made. God showed up and asked us to trust him through our fear. "It is I," he said. "You can trust me. Do not be afraid. I've got this."

Acts 6:1–7
Psalm 33:1–2,4–5,18–19
John 6:16–21

*The two disciples recounted what had taken place on the way, and how
Jesus was made known to them in the breaking of bread.*
—LUKE 24:35

After his Resurrection, Jesus appeared to the disciples and ate
with them. He shows us his humanity by submitting to his
human need for food. Jesus asked them, "Have you anything
here to eat?" And they gave him a piece of baked fish. But his
actions also symbolize our divine hunger and need for
spiritual food. Jesus told the disciples, "These are my words
that I spoke to you while I was still with you, that everything
written about me in the law of Moses and in the prophets
and psalms must be fulfilled." Then he opened their minds to
help them understand the Scriptures. Jesus eats with us to
show us his humanity, and he fills us spiritually to show us
his divinity.

Acts 3:13–15,17–19
Psalm 4:2,4,7–8,9 (7a)
1 John 2:1–5a
Luke 24:35–48

"Amen, amen, I say to you, you are looking for me not because you saw signs but because you ate the loaves and were filled."
—JOHN 6:26

Only God can satisfy. Why do we insist on looking elsewhere for our contentment—in our jobs, our looks, our children, our successes? As Blaise Pascal writes in *Pensées*, "This he tries in vain to fill with everything around him, seeking in things that are not there the help he cannot find in those that are, though none can help, since this infinite abyss can be filled only with an infinite and immutable object; in other words by God himself."

Acts 6:8–15
Psalm 119:23–24,26–27,29–30
John 6:22–29

Tuesday

APRIL 17

"You always oppose the Holy Spirit."
—ACTS 7:51

Sometimes I get nudges from the Holy Spirit and ignore them. I get too busy or afraid. I take things into my own hands because I think I know what I'm doing, and it never turns out well. When you sense the Holy Spirit's leading, don't ignore it. I've heard this called "cooperating with grace." The Holy Spirit wants to lead us into things that are life-giving and freeing. Don't miss out.

Acts 7:51—8:1a
Psalm 31:3cd–4,6 and 7b and 8a,17 and 21ab
John 6:30–35

APRIL 18

There broke out a severe persecution of the Church in Jerusalem, and all were scattered.

—ACTS 8:1

Throughout history, Christians have been persecuted in places such as Japan, Iraq, Syria, and North Korea. The 1966 novel *Silence* by Shusaku Endo explores the spiritual struggles of a Jesuit priest amid the severe persecution of Japanese Christians. As he watches Japanese Christians being hung upside down and bled to death, he wonders why God is silent. In the end, he concludes, "But our Lord was not silent. Even if he had been silent, my life until this day would have spoken of Him." He senses God saying to him, "When you suffer, I suffer with you. To the end I am close to you." Pray today for those Christians who are experiencing persecution, that they may sense God's presence too.

Acts 8:1b–8
Psalm 66:1–3a,4–5,6–7a
John 6:35–40

*"I am the living bread that came down from heaven; whoever eats this
bread will live forever; and the bread that I will give is my Flesh for the
life of the world."*
—JOHN 6:51

There's something about bread that is sustaining, life-giving,
comforting, and filling. To me, it just speaks of "home." I still
remember the smell of the Swedish limpa bread my mother
used to make. And when I went to Paris a few years ago, I
lived on the baguettes that were baked fresh every morning.
Not surprisingly, over and over again, Christ is described as
"bread." And just like bread, Jesus sustains us, comforts us,
gives us life, and is our home.

Acts 8:26–40
Psalm 66:8–9,16–17,20
John 6:44–51

Friday
APRIL 20

"Whoever eats my Flesh and drinks my Blood has eternal life, and I will raise him on the last day. For my Flesh is true food, and my Blood is true drink."
—JOHN 6:54–55

My favorite part of Mass is watching other congregants walking up to accept the Eucharist. I watch as young, old, black, white, rich, and poor walk toward life, hope, and resurrection. I often think that maybe some of them are just doing it out of habit or because it's what they're "supposed to do." Maybe to some it's a ritual they learned as children. But maybe to others it is the one thing that is sustaining them—what gives them hope. Either way, something is compelling each person to walk up to the table to eat his Flesh and drink his Blood. To accept this life-saving gift being offered.

Acts 9:1–20
Psalm 117:1bc,2
John 6:52–59

Jesus then said to the Twelve, "Do you also want to leave?" Simon Peter
answered him, "Master, to whom shall we go?"
—JOHN 6:67–68

I was laid off from my job in 2009 during the recession. My husband was in school and only working part-time. The economy was dead; there were no jobs to be found. Even freelance projects were few and far between. I did not know how we would survive financially. All I could think to do was to pray. When we are at the end of our resources, the only place we can turn to is God. The disciples are saying, *We have nowhere else to go. You're our only hope.* There's something freeing about surrender. We try and try to make everything work, but sometimes we just have to throw up our hands and say, "Help, God! You're my only hope!"

Acts 9:31–42
Psalm 116:12–13,14–15,16–17
John 6:60–69

Sunday

APRIL 22

• FOURTH SUNDAY OF EASTER •

Beloved, we are God's children now; what we shall be has not yet been revealed.
—1 JOHN 3:2

I love watching my daughter learn and grow. She's six, and she's starting to read and form strong opinions. She does not like songs that are quiet; she likes songs that are loud and upbeat. She loves to dance and ice skate and swim. She doesn't like being too hot or in the sun too long. She is outgoing and has a lot of friends. Her teachers tell us that she is a leader. Like a Polaroid picture, she's slowly developing before our very eyes. Likewise, we are God's children, being formed slowly and surely into the people God has created us to be, but the final picture has not yet been revealed.

Acts 4:8–12
Psalm 118:1,8–9,21–23,26,28,29
1 John 3:1–2
John 10:11–18

• ST. GEORGE, MARTYR * ST. ADALBERT, BISHOP AND MARTYR •

Send forth your light and your fidelity;
they shall lead me on.
—PSALM 43:3

This passage reminds me of the Thomas Merton prayer from
his book *Thoughts in Solitude*: "My Lord God, I have no idea
where I am going. I do not see the road ahead of me. I
cannot know for certain where it will end. . . . The fact that I
think that I am following your will does not mean that I am
actually doing so. But I believe that the desire to please you
does in fact please you. . . . I hope that I will never do
anything apart from that desire. And I know that if I do this
you will lead me by the right road though I may know
nothing about it. Therefore will I trust you always though I
may seem to be lost and in the shadow of death. I will not
fear, for you are ever with me."

Acts 11:1–18
Psalm 42:2–3; 43:3–4
John 10:1–10

"My sheep hear my voice; I know them, and they follow me."
—JOHN 10:27

"Stop the noise and you will hear his voice in silence," the poet Rumi wrote. I have been practicing meditation lately, sitting in silence to hear God's still, quiet voice. It's difficult to sit in silence. I started at five minutes and now I'm up to ten minutes. My goal is twenty minutes. But with so many voices in my head, how can I hear God? I run through the list of things I have to do. I fight off worry and anxiety. I hear my neighbor outside tending to his yard and think about how I need to do the same. I get distracted and bored. But I'm determined to stick it out and learn how to be still. Because I'm desperate to hear God's voice and go where he leads.

Acts 11:19–26
Psalm 87:1b–3,4–5,6–7
John 10:22–30

Wednesday

APRIL 25

• ST. MARK, EVANGELIST •

Then the Lord Jesus, after he spoke to them, was taken up into heaven and took his seat at the right hand of God. But they went forth and preached everywhere, while the Lord worked with them and confirmed the word through accompanying signs.
—MARK 16:19–20

We are the hands and feet of Jesus. We are called to go forth and spread the Good News of the Gospel. If not through our words, then through our actions. How are you being the hands and feet of Jesus today?

1 Peter 5:5b–14
Psalm 89:2–3,6–7,16–17
Mark 16:15–20

Thursday

APRIL 26

When Jesus had washed the disciples' feet, he said to them: "Amen, amen,
I say to you, no slave is greater than his master nor any messenger
greater than the one who sent him."
—JOHN 13:16

In Jesus' day, the disciples' feet must have been dusty and
smelly. They wore sandals, walked everywhere, and didn't
have the advantage of foot powder. So for Jesus to lean down
and wash their feet was a great act of humility and love. He
was the Messiah, and yet he was humble enough to wash the
soles of his followers. How are you serving others today? If
you're in a position of leadership, how are you humbly
serving those who are in positions under you?

Acts 13:13–25
Psalm 89:2–3,21–22,25 and 27
John 13:16–20

"Do not let your hearts be troubled."
—JOHN 14:1

I come from a family of handwringers. Literally, we twist our
hands in knots when we're anxious. To this day my father,
now eighty-five, worries when my family and I travel. He
tells us to call him as soon as we get home. I remember him
checking every lock on the doors to our house twice at night,
fretting until we made it home from youth group, and
hesitating to let us travel overseas in college. We pass along
our fears to our children, and sure enough, all of us kids are
anxious. I've tried to overcome anxiety, which has affected
my career and my family, through medication and therapy.
Christ says that we should not let our hearts be troubled. We
need to stop wringing our hands and have faith that God will
take care of us.

Acts 13:26–33
Psalm 2:6–7,8–9,10–11
John 14:1–6

• ST. PETER CHANEL, PRIEST AND MARTYR * ST. LOUIS GRIGNION
DE MONTFORT, PRIEST •

"Whoever has seen me has seen the Father."
—JOHN 14:9

In the Anne Sexton poem "The Big Heart," she writes,
"Though there are times of doubt . . . / still God is filling me."
When we hit rock-bottom, God fills us, but only when we
have exhausted our own resources, our own ego, our own
idea of what we and our lives should be like. Only when we
are at our wits' end, when we can no longer hold up all the
spinning plates, is there room for God to fill us with himself.
Only then can we totally reflect the love of God, and, as it
says in 1 John 3:2–3, we shall be like him because we shall
see him as he is.

Acts 13:44–52
Psalm 98:1,2–3ab,3cd–4
John 14:7–14

APRIL 29

• FIFTH SUNDAY OF EASTER •

Children, let us love not in word or speech but in deed and truth.
—1 JOHN 3:18

Integrity means adhering to a moral code or set of values. But it also means being complete or undivided. We all know people who say one thing and do another. But integrity means saying and doing the same thing. Lord, let us love not just in our words but in our actions as well.

Acts 9:26–31
Psalm 22:26–27,28,30,31–32
1 John 3:18–24
John 15:1–8

———————

"We proclaim to you good news that you should turn from these idols to the living God, who made heaven and earth and sea and all that is in them."
—ACTS 14:15

If I could, I would live by the sea. There's something about the ocean, the warm sand, the sound of the waves, the vastness of it stretching to the horizon. The only place I can nap is on the beach, where the waves lull me to sleep. I have seen whales breaching in the Pacific, and I have sailed in the Caribbean. I've watched baby sea turtles hatch from their eggs in the sand in Mexico and push their way to the water, where they swim for miles and live for one hundred years. I'm in awe. How can we worship our puny idols instead of the God who has created earth and the sea and everything in them?

Acts 14:5–18
Psalm 115:1–2,3–4,15–16
John 14:21–26

Tuesday

MAY 1

• ST. JOSEPH THE WORKER •

They stoned Paul and dragged him out of the city, supposing that he was dead. But when the disciples gathered around him, he got up and entered the city.
—ACTS 14:19–20

"When the disciples gathered around him . . ." Paul had been stoned and left for dead, and his community came around him and helped until he could get up and go on his way. We live in a society that idealizes the rugged individual who can make it on his or her own. But we all need each other. After my mom died, I remember clearly the people who came to the house to drop off food and embrace us. Friends from our old church whom I hadn't seen in years showed up with tuna casseroles, six-packs of Coke, pans of lasagna. When they gathered around us, we eventually had the strength to get up and start walking again.

Acts 14:19–28
Psalm 145:10–11,12–13ab,21
John 14:27–31a (or, for the Memorial,
Genesis 1:26—2:3 or
Colossians 3:14–15,17,23–24)
Psalm 90:2,3–4,12–13,14 and 16
Matthew 13:54–58

• ST. ATHANASIUS, BISHOP AND DOCTOR OF THE CHURCH •

*"I am the true vine, and my Father is the vine grower. He takes away
every branch in me that does not bear fruit."*
—JOHN 15:1–2

On my back deck, I keep flower pots filled with petunias and
pansies. After work I go out to the deck to water the flowers
and pick off any dead petals, making room for new ones to
bloom. I've always thought this passage of Scripture was
brutal—with Jesus talking about pruning us and taking away
the branches that do not bear fruit. And yet when I think of
the little flowers on my deck, I remove the dead petals out of
love and care. I want the plants to become full and beautiful
and healthy. When God prunes away all that is keeping us
from growing, he does it gently, caringly, lovingly, because
he wants us to grow strong and beautiful.

Acts 15:1–6
Psalm 122:1–2,3–4ab,4cd–5
John 15:1–8

Thursday

MAY 3

• SS. PHILIP AND JAMES, APOSTLES •

"I am the way and the truth and the life."
—JOHN 14:6

How often do we doubt God's love? How many times do we
question our own worthiness? How many times do we take
control of our own lives because we do not think God knows
what's best for us? Martin Luther wrote, "The sin underneath
all our sins is to trust the lie of the serpent that we cannot
trust the love and grace of Christ and must take matters into
our own hands." *God loves you. God loves you. God loves you.*
When will you believe it?

1 Corinthians 15:1–8
Psalm 19:2–3,4–5
John 14:6–14

Friday

MAY 4

"This is my commandment: love one another as I love you. No one has greater love than this, to lay down one's life for one's friends."
—JOHN 15:12–13

We all hear heroic stories of soldiers getting killed as they try to save their fellow soldiers—think *Saving Private Ryan*. But we too lay down our lives for those around us every day—even if it isn't so dramatic and cinematic. We sacrifice for those we love, whether it's a spouse, a child, or an elderly parent. We give away pieces of ourselves, our time, our energy, our money. It's these small, heroic acts that add up to great love. How are you laying down your life for your friends today?

Acts 15:22–31
Psalm 57:8–9,10 and 12
John 15:12–17

⇒ 153 ⇐

"If you belonged to the world, the world would love its own; but because you do not belong to the world, and I have chosen you out of the world, the world hates you."
—JOHN 15:19

If you are a follower of Christ, you will often find yourself in situations where your values and priorities are different from those who do not believe. Someone who wants to climb the corporate ladder at all costs may despise you for working to bring compassion and care into the workplace. Someone who desires riches for his or her own glory may look down on your message of giving alms to the poor. Being a Christian means being a voice in the wilderness. We have been chosen to preach the Good News.

Acts 16:1–10
Psalm 100:1–2,3,5
John 15:18–21

Whoever is without love does not know God, for God is love.
—1 JOHN 4:8

Throughout history, people have tried to make Christianity
about politics, about power, about wars, about being right,
about theology, about prosperity, about judgment. But they
have been wrong. Christianity is about love. Pure and simple.

Acts 10:25–26,34–35,44–48
Psalm 98:1,2–3,3–4
1 John 4:7–10
John 15:9–17

*"And you also testify, because you have been with me from
the beginning."*
—JOHN 15:27

I come from a family of storytellers. I grew up listening to my
dad and uncle, both in their 80s now, tell stories of their
childhood growing up on a farm in Iowa. I also spent hours
in church pews listening to the testimonies of congregants in
the little Baptist church that my ancestors founded. Joan
Didion, in her collection of short stories *The White Album*,
writes, "We tell ourselves stories in order to live." In this
Scripture passage, Jesus urges his disciples to tell the stories
of his life, death, and Resurrection. To testify—to give
evidence, bear witness—so that others may know what Jesus
has done and find life through him.

Acts 16:11–15
Psalm 149:1b–2,3–4,5–6a and 9b
John 15:26—16:4a

*When the jailer woke up and saw the prison doors wide open, he drew his
sword and was about to kill himself, thinking that the prisoners had
escaped. But Paul shouted out in a loud voice, "Do no harm to yourself;
we are all here."*
—ACTS 16:27–28

The jailer puts Paul and Silas in the innermost jail cell and
secures their feet to a stake. But then things start getting
weird. First Paul and Silas are singing in prison. Who sings in
the midst of suffering? Then there is the earthquake. Finally,
just when the jailer is about to kill himself, Paul shouts to
him—Stop! Don't do it! "We are all here." The jailer rushes in
and begs to be saved. Was it the singing, or the earthquake,
or the act of grace from Paul that prompted the jailer to want
to be saved? Whatever it was, the jailer knew something was
up. It was powerful and life-giving. And he wanted to be
part of it.

Acts 16:22–34
Psalm 138:1–2ab,2cde–3,7c–8
John 16:5–11

He fixed the ordered seasons and the boundaries of their regions, so that people might seek God, even perhaps grope for him and find him, though indeed he is not far from any one of us.

—ACTS 17:26–27

In the dark night of the soul, when all seems lost, I grope for God. I feel my way in the dark, desperate for a sign that he is near. In this passage, Paul is telling the Athenians that their religion, shrines, and sanctuaries are not where God dwells.

He says, "Rather it is he who gives to everyone life and breath and everything." Indeed, God is not far from any one of us. Sometimes we just need to be reminded, and believe, that he is near.

Acts 17:15,22—18:1
Psalm 148:1–2,11–12,13,14
John 16:12–15

Thursday

MAY 10

• THE ASCENSION OF THE LORD • ST. DAMIEN DE VEUSTER, PRIEST •

"It is not for you to know the times or seasons that the Father has established by his own authority. But you will receive power when the Holy Spirit comes upon you."
—ACTS 1:7–8

Growing up fundamentalist, we were obsessed with when Christ would return. Sometimes a popular evangelist would even come up with a date for the "rapture"—when all of those who were saved would be taken up to heaven, leaving the rest of the poor souls on earth to suffer. Many nights I would lie awake on the bottom bunk of my bunk bed and pray over and over again for God to forgive my sins and save me. I didn't want to be left behind. And of course, that date for the rapture would come and go and we'd still be here. I'd spend much of my life waiting for something to happen, for God to appear. I later realized he had been with me all along.

MAY 11

"Do not be afraid. Go on speaking, and do not be silent, for I am with you."
—ACTS 18:9–10

Noli timere. Those were the last words the poet Seamus Heaney wrote in a text to his wife. They mean "Don't be afraid" in Latin. Long before Seamus Heaney said those words to his wife, Jesus said them to Paul in a vision: "Do not be afraid. Go on speaking. . . . I'm with you."

Acts 18:9–18
Psalm 47:2–3,4–5,6–7
John 16:20–23

Saturday

MAY 12

"Amen, amen, I say to you, whatever you ask the Father in my name he will give you."
—JOHN 16:23

Does this verse mean that Jesus will give us anything we want, if we only ask in his name? Surely not, because we all know this is not how God works. And let's be honest: aren't we often relieved when God does not always give us what we want? God is too big for the small boxes we put him in. Our imaginations are too trite. We want what we want, but God's plans for us are much bigger than we can imagine.

Acts 18:23–28
Psalm 47:2–3,8–9,10
John 16:23b–28

Sunday

MAY 13

• THE ASCENSION OF THE LORD • SEVENTH SUNDAY OF EASTER •

"Holy Father, keep them in your name that you have given me, so that they may be one just as we are one."
—JOHN 17:11

These days, there is more division among Christians than I have ever seen in my lifetime. In the most recent presidential election, it was hard for me to understand how Christians could have such different views on issues. But Jesus wants us to "be one." How can we go about doing that? Maybe we can start by reaching out to those who think differently than we do and try to understand their perspective.

SEVENTH SUNDAY OF EASTER:
Acts 1:15–17,20a,20c–26
1 John 4:11–16
John 17:11b–19

THE ASCENSION OF THE LORD:
Acts 1:1–11
Psalm 47:2–3,6–7,8–9 (6)
Ephesians 1:17–23 or 4:1–13 or 4:1–7,11–13
Mark 16:15–20

Monday

MAY 14

• ST. MATTHIAS, APOSTLE •

"As the Father loves me, so I also love you. Remain in my love."
—JOHN 15:9

My church sponsors a retreat three times a year called the Beloved Retreat. The first time I attended, I had no idea what to expect. I was nervous. I didn't know anyone. But from the time I unloaded my suitcase and walked into the retreat center until I left a few days later, I was overwhelmed with acts of kindness and love. The whole weekend is designed to help participants know, as God said to Jesus at his baptism, "You are my beloved son; with you I am well pleased." (NAB Mark 1:11) We often forget that God loves us, and it's up to us to remind each other that we are truly his Beloved.

Acts 1:15–17,20–26
Psalm 113:1–2,3–4,5–6,7–8
John 15:9–17

MAY 15

• ST. ISIDORE •

*"I glorified you on earth by accomplishing the work that you
gave me to do."*
—JOHN 17:4

In his book *Wishful Thinking*, Frederick Buechner writes, "The
place God calls you to is the place where your deep gladness
and the world's deep hunger meet." I have often struggled
with following my calling, particularly when I know the
sacrifices, especially financial, that I will need to make to
follow that call wholeheartedly. But today's Scripture reminds
me: we glorify God on earth by accomplishing the work that
God gives us to do. Lord, give me the courage to
follow my call.

Acts 20:17–27
Psalm 68:10–11,20–21
John 17:1–11a

Wednesday

MAY 16

*"We must help the weak, and keep in mind the words of the Lord Jesus
who himself said, 'It is more blessed to give than to receive.'"*
—ACTS 20:35

So much of parenting is just a guessing game—wondering if
you're instilling kindness, compassion, and courage into your
children—that it's hard to know if you're doing it right. This
is especially difficult around Christmas and birthdays, when
it seems like it's all about the gifts. Since Desta is the
youngest grandchild, aunts, uncles, and grandparents spoil
her regularly. So my heart jumped the other day when she
asked me for a dollar to give to a homeless man. Now she
regularly notices the homeless on the streets, wondering if
they have enough to eat and asking me where they will sleep.
She's learning the blessings of helping the weak and giving
instead of receiving.

Acts 20:28–38
Psalm 68:29–30,33–35a,35bc–36ab
John 17:11b–19

MAY 17

*"I pray not only for these, but also for those who will believe in me
through their word, so that they may all be one . . . that the world may
believe that you sent me."*
—JOHN 17:20–21

I remember when I was twelve years old, our congregation
was milling about on the lawn outside after a church business
meeting on a warm summer evening when we heard a scuffle.
I looked over, and two deacons were having a fistfight on the
front lawn. Men from the congregation broke up the fight,
and my parents herded us kids into my dad's brown Cadillac.
We never went back to that church. My wise parents knew
that they wanted something different—that Christianity
wasn't about fighting over things like what color carpet
should be laid in the sanctuary. The world will know us by
our love, not by our fistfights.

Acts 22:30; 23:6–11
Psalm 16:1–2a and 5,7–8,9–10,11
John 17:20–26

Friday

MAY 18

*"Simon, son of John, do you love me more than these?" Simon Peter
answered him, "Yes, Lord, you know that I love you." Jesus said to him,
"Feed my lambs."*

—JOHN 21:15

Jesus asks Simon Peter if he loves him three times. Each time,
Simon Peter answers yes, and Jesus responds by giving him
an action to take: feed my lambs, tend my sheep, feed my
sheep. At the end of the passage, Jesus tells him, "Follow me."
Love isn't just a feeling or something we say; it's an action.
Jesus wants us to show that we love him by tending his sheep
and feeding his lambs. We need to go out and do good in the
world. Love Jesus by taking action.

Acts 25:13b–21
Psalm 103:1–2,11–12,19–20ab
John 21:15–19

"You follow me."
—JOHN 21:22

When I was young, I would listen to missionaries tell stories about their adventures and struggles in a faraway land. Often their stories would include how they "followed Christ" by giving up everything to become a missionary. I worried that I would have to move to a hut in a foreign country to follow Christ. Instead, I would move to an apartment in Chicago. But every day I ask myself if I am following Christ. Am I willing to give up my security, comfort, and wealth to follow him? Am I willing to do something scary to fulfill my calling? I often choose comfort and security, but then realize how much I am missing out.

Acts 28:16–20,30–31
Psalm 11:4,5 and 7
John 21:20–25

"I have much more to tell you, but you cannot bear it now. But when he comes, the Spirit of truth, he will guide you to all truth."
—JOHN 16:12–13

Even the disciples did not understand everything that Jesus was saying or what was going to happen, and so he sent the Holy Spirit to guide them and reveal the truth to them in time. We, too, do not understand yet and need the help of the Holy Spirit. Jesus calls him the "Paraclete," which means "the one who comes to our aid." The Holy Spirit will guide us to all truth. Pope Francis reminds us that we need to pray "Holy Spirit may my heart be open to the Word of God, may my heart be open to good, may my heart be open to the beauty of God, every day."

VIGIL:
Genesis 11:1–9 or Exodus 19:3–8,16–20b or
Ezekiel 37:1–4 or Joel 3:1–5
Psalm 104:1–2,24,35,27–28,29,30
Romans 8:22–27
John 7:37–39

DAY:
Acts 2:1–11
Psalm 104:1,24,29–30,31,34
1 Corinthians 12:3b–7,12–13 or
Galatians 5:16–25
John 20:19–23 or 15:26–27; 16:12–15

Monday

MAY 21

Beloved: Who among you is wise and understanding? Let him show his works by a good life in the humility that comes from wisdom. But if you have bitter jealousy and selfish ambition in your hearts, do not boast and be false to the truth.
—JAMES 3:13–14

I have worked for many years in the business world, creating websites, advertisements, and marketing materials for various companies. It's creative and pays the bills. But the business world is filled with people who are bitterly jealous and selfishly ambitious and who lie just to get ahead. It's easy to throw character out the window for short-term gain. But following Christ sometimes means giving up short-term gain for something much greater. The martyrs knew this and paid for it with their lives. We may have to sacrifice a promotion or wealth, but living a good life in humility and wisdom makes it well worth it.

James 3:13–18
Psalm 19:8,9,10,15
Mark 9:14–29

"If anyone wishes to be first, he shall be the last of all and the servant of all."
—MARK 9:35

The disciples were arguing about which of them was the greatest. Jesus' reply to their discussion was not what they expected. He told them that the last shall be first, and anyone who wants to be great will be a servant of all. This is typical of Jesus' message—he's always turning things on their head. The kingdom of God is the opposite of the ways of the world. If you want to be great, Jesus says, humble yourself and serve others. St. Augustine wrote, "Do you wish to rise? Begin by descending. You plan a tower that will pierce the clouds? Lay first the foundation of humility."

James 4:1–10
Psalm 55:7–8,9–10a,10b–11a,23
Mark 9:30–37

Wednesday

MAY 23

*"You have no idea what your life will be like tomorrow. You are a puff of
smoke that appears briefly and then disappears. Instead you should say,
'If the Lord wills it, we shall live to do this or that.'"*
—JAMES 4:14–15

I remember it clearly: It was a rainy April night during my
senior year of college, and I was studying in my dorm room. I
heard a commotion outside the door, and when I opened it, I
found out there had been a car accident. One of my best
friends was in the hospital with a shattered face, and two
other friends were dead. My friend survived, but he had
months of recovery ahead. For the first time, I understood
how brief this life can be. Our lives are truly in God's hands.
Let us ask ourselves every day: how can we make it count?

James 4:13–17
Psalm 49:2–3,6–7,8–10,11
Mark 9:38–40

Fear not when a man grows rich,
when the wealth of his house becomes great,
For when he dies, he shall take none of it;
his wealth shall not follow him down.
—PSALM 49:17–18

In the 1938 movie *You Can't Take It with You*, a rich family spurns the family of their son's girlfriend because they are poor and eccentric. The wealthy father, a successful banker, ruthlessly buys up a whole neighborhood just to put his competitor out of business. The girlfriend's grandfather tells him at one point, "Maybe it'd stop you trying to be so desperate about making more money than you can ever use? You can't take it with you, Mr. Kirby. So what good is it? As near as I can see, the only thing you can take with you is the love of your friends." As written in Matthew 6:21, where your treasure is, that's where your heart is.

James 5:1–6
Psalm 49:14–15ab,15cd–16,17–18,19–20
Mark 9:41–50

• ST. BEDE THE VENERABLE, PRIEST AND DOCTOR OF THE CHURCH •
ST. GREGORY VII, POPE • ST. MARY MAGDALENE DE' PAZZI, VIRGIN •

*Do not complain, brothers and sisters, about one another, that you may
not be judged. Behold, the Judge is standing before the gates.*
—JAMES 5:9

It's hard not to judge other people. I often go through my
days making judgments. But through the years, as I've
become more aware of my own failings and weaknesses, I've
realized that my judgments say more about me than they do
about the person I'm judging. Henri Nouwen writes, "As long
as we continue to live as if we are what we do, what we have,
and what other people think about us, we will remain filled
with judgments, opinions, evaluations, and condemnations.
We will remain addicted to putting people and things in their
'right' place."

James 5:9–12
Psalm 103:1–2,3–4,8–9,11–12
Mark 10:1–12

*"Amen, I say to you, whoever does not accept the Kingdom of God like a
child will not enter it."*
—MARK 10:15

I'm often too exhausted to pray with my daughter before
bedtime. But a few weeks ago, when I was going through a
stressful time at work and was drained and discouraged, she
said, out of the blue at bedtime, "Mommy, let's pray!" Desta
kneeled at the side of the bed and made me kneel too. She
made the sign of the cross, and then she started
praying—thanking God for her family, and her school, and
her house, and that we had adopted her. Her prayer went on
and on and soon I was thanking God too.

James 5:13–20
Psalm 141:1–2,3 and 8
Mark 10:13–16

For you did not receive a spirit of slavery to fall back into fear, but you received a Spirit of adoption, through whom we cry, "Abba, Father!"
—ROMANS 8:15

I look at Desta's brown skin next to my white skin and wonder what it all means. How did we become a family? How did a girl whose ancestors were slaves in Mississippi, who came to Chicago during the Great Migration, get adopted by parents whose ancestors came from Sweden and Scotland? I may spend the rest of my life trying to understand it, and Desta may spend the rest of her life making peace with it. Once in Mass, Desta whispered to me, much too loudly, "Mommy, did you know that God is everybody's daddy?" I smiled and nodded my head. However she comes to understand our story, I hope she will always find comfort in her Abba, Father.

Deuteronomy 4:32–34,39–40
Psalm 33:4–5,6,9,18–19,20,22 (12b)
Romans 8:14–17
Matthew 28:16–20

Monday

MAY 28

"Go, sell what you have, and give to the poor and you will have treasure
in heaven; then come, follow me."
—MARK 10:21

I used to have a white Crate and Barrel couch and love seat
that I bought secondhand from a friend. The couches were in
pristine condition when I got them, but then I got married
and adopted our daughter, and soon the couches were
stained and tattered. The white slipcovers were ripped and
torn, and buying new slipcovers would have cost as much as
buying a new couch. And yet, I couldn't part with them.
Why is it so hard to give up our possessions? I often cling to
what I have, afraid of change or paralyzed by sentiment. But
in order to move into a new life, we need to give up the old. I
finally sold the couches on Craigslist and bought a new IKEA
gray sectional.

1 Peter 1:3–9
Psalm 111:1–2,5–6,9 and 10c
Mark 10:17–27

Tuesday

MAY 29

Set your hopes completely on the grace to be brought to you at the revelation of Jesus Christ.
—1 PETER 1:13

Grace is waking up sick and depressed and then hearing the joy in your daughter's voice when she reads a book for the first time. Grace is feeling like a failure at work but then having a coworker send you a note thanking you for a job well done. Grace is hearing the doorbell ring and seeing the faces of unexpected friends in the doorway. Grace is seeing the sun peek through the clouds after days and days of rain. Grace is lamenting the state of your life yet feeling subtle shifts inside you, pulling you closer to God. Let us set our hopes on these things that blow into our lives as unpredictably as the wind.

1 Peter 1:10–16
Psalm 98:1,2–3ab,3cd–4
Mark 10:28–31

Wednesday

MAY 30

"All flesh is like grass,
and all its glory like the flower of the field;
the grass withers,
and the flower wilts;
but the word of the Lord remains forever."
—1 PETER 1:24,25

Every once in a while, Scripture reminds us of how small and temporary we are. We are like the grass that withers and the flower that wilts. It's not very encouraging. But in this passage's previous verse, we are also reminded that we have "been born anew, not from perishable but from imperishable seed, through the living and abiding word of God." (1 Peter 1:23) Right now my hydrangeas are blooming outside, and the grass is green, being born anew just like we will be someday.

1 Peter 1:18–25
Psalm 147:12–13,14–15,19–20
Mark 10:32–45

Mary set out and traveled to the hill country in haste to a town of Judah, where she entered the house of Zechariah and greeted Elizabeth.
—LUKE 1:39–40

As soon as Mary was informed by the angel that she was going to give birth to the Christ child, she went in haste to see the elderly Elizabeth, who was also pregnant. Both had been visited by angels who had told them of their unlikely pregnancies and commanded them not to be afraid. Surely, they found comfort in each other, knowing someone else was experiencing the same fear, excitement, and mystery. Someone else who could understand. Do you often try to go through difficult times on your own, hunkering down and isolating yourself? I know I do. But when God puts someone in our path who can understand our struggles, we can accept that grace for what it is.

Zephaniah 3:14–18a or Romans 12:9–16
Isaiah 12:2–3,4bcd,5–6
Luke 1:39–56

But rejoice to the extent that you share in the sufferings of Christ, so that when his glory is revealed you may also rejoice exultantly.
—1 PETER 4:13

I grew up believing that Christ's death was a substitution for our own—that it was a "payment" for our sins. But much later in life I heard another view of Christ's death—that it wasn't about Christ paying a penalty, it was about God's victory over sin and death. God conquers death by fully entering into it. Thus, the crucifixion is not a necessary transaction to appease a wrathful and justice-demanding deity but an act of divine love. God enters into our suffering with us. We participate with him in his suffering, and that is the beauty of the paschal mystery: we participate in Christ's life, death, and Resurrection every day.

1 Peter 4:7–13
Psalm 96:10,11–12,13
Mark 11:11–26

The chief priests, the scribes, and the elders approached him and said to him, "By what authority are you doing these things? Or who gave you this authority to do them?"
—MARK 11:27–28

The religious leaders doubted Jesus. Who gave him the right to perform miracles and spread his message of salvation? In response, Jesus asked them, "Was John's baptism of heavenly or of human origin?" The leaders waffled, not wanting to commit either way. It was a catch-22. If they said heavenly origin, they knew Jesus would then ask them why they didn't believe him. If they said human origin, they were afraid it would upset the crowd, who thought John was a prophet. Finally, they said, "We do not know." When Jesus asks us to believe in him, what is our response? Do we waffle? Or do we say that he is the Son of God, our Lord, our Savior?

Jude 17,20b–25
Psalm 63:2,3–4,5–6
Mark 11:27–33

Sunday

JUNE 3

• THE MOST HOLY BODY AND BLOOD OF CHRIST (CORPUS CHRISTI) •

*While they were eating, he took bread, said the blessing, broke it, gave it
to them, and said, "Take it; this is my body."*
—MARK 14:22

Jesus ate with everyone—the tax collectors, the sinners, the
prostitutes—and it drove the Jewish authorities nuts because
it went against their laws. But dining with others was a
central characteristic of his ministry. His life was a moveable
feast. His dinner parties symbolized the kingdom,
forgiveness, and the relationships possible in Jesus. The Last
Supper is the culmination of this "table ministry," and when
we take the Eucharist, we should ask ourselves: are we
becoming more inclusive, more hospitable, and more
forgiving?

Exodus 24:3–8
Psalm 116:12–13,15–16,17–18
Hebrews 9:11–15
Mark 14:12–16,22–26

Monday

JUNE 4

*"My refuge and my fortress,
my God, in whom I trust."*
—PSALM 91:2

I have been waiting most of my life. I didn't marry until I was
39. It took seven years for us to adopt a child. And I just
learned I'll have to wait a year or more for my condo to sell.
First World problem to be sure. And yet there are reasons for
our desire to move: more room for our work, more space to
entertain guests, and another room to possibly welcome
another foster child into our home. God knows our longings.
He knows the desires of our hearts and the pain of our
waiting. Too often, I don't trust that God knows what he is
doing. That there is a purpose to our pain, even in the pain
of waiting.

2 Peter 1:2–7
Psalm 91:1–2,14–15b,15c–16
Mark 12:1–12

JUNE 5

• ST. BONIFACE, BISHOP AND MARTYR •

Seventy is the sum of our years,
or eighty, if we are strong,
And most of them are fruitless toil,
for they pass quickly and we drift away.
Fill us at daybreak with your kindness,
that we may shout for joy and gladness all our days.
—PSALM 90:10,14

The older I get, the more quickly time passes. Life speeds by like I'm on an Amtrak train, watching the miles blur past in a collage of sky and land and clouds. I want to catch the days, sometimes, and hang on to them. And yet the train keeps moving. *Stop.* I think. *Stop the train.* Let me take it all in. The warmth of my husband's touch and the twinkle in my daughter's eyes. The sun on my face and the smell of morning coffee. Don't let me miss these small moments of joy.

2 Peter 3:12–15a,17–18
Psalm 90:2,3–4,10,14 and 16
Mark 12:13–17

Wednesday
JUNE 6
• ST. NORBERT, BISHOP •

For God did not give us a spirit of cowardice but rather of power and love and self-control.
—2 TIMOTHY 1:7

Throughout my life, I have been paralyzed by social anxiety. I didn't talk until I was four. My heart races when I have to give a presentation at work. I stand by the door at parties wondering when it will be time to leave. I've spent much of my life trying to overcome my anxiety and fear. What could I accomplish if I fully embraced the power, love, and self-control that comes from God? What about you? What are you afraid of today?

2 Timothy 1:1–3,6–12
Psalm 123:1b–2ab,2cdef
Mark 12:18–27

Thursday

JUNE 7

"You shall love the Lord your God with all your heart, with all your
soul, with all your mind, and with all your strength."
—MARK 12:30–31

Jesus said that the greatest commandment is to love the Lord,
and the second is to love your neighbor. If this is true, then
why do we Christians argue with one another, judge others,
and ignore those next door? The Christian faith really comes
down to love. If we aren't loving God and loving others, then
what are we doing?

2 Timothy 2:8–15
Psalm 25:4–5ab,8–9,10 and 14
Mark 12:28–34

My heart is overwhelmed,
my pity is stirred.
—HOSEA 11:8

The centurions at the cross pierced his side, and water and
blood and love flowed out. He was already gone. Dead. So
they didn't have to break his legs as they did for the criminals
on either side of him. His heart had stopped beating, at least
for now. It had been spent: the miracles, the healings, his
love for the crowds and the twelve. He gave everything,
down to the last pulse of his heart. As the beat of love flowed
out into the world, his disciples and Mary and his followers
grieved. But then they got up and started carrying this love
to the ends of the earth.

Hosea 11:1,3–4,8c–9
Isaiah 12:2–3,4,5–6
Ephesians 3:8–12,14–19
John 19:31–37

I rejoice heartily in the LORD,
in my God is the joy of my soul.
—ISAIAH 61:10 (FROM FEAST DAY READING)

My husband calls me a "dour Swede." I wish I were more chipper. I have a friend who never allows herself to dip into sadness. She puts a positive spin on everything. That's not healthy, but I do know that God wants us to have joy. Joy is a constant theme throughout Scripture. Philippians 4:4 says, "Rejoice in the Lord always. I shall say it again: rejoice!" And 1 Thessalonians 5:16 says, "Rejoice always." Today's reading tells us that God has clothed us with a robe of salvation, and as the earth brings forth its plants, so will the Lord God make justice and praise spring up before all the nations. That's a message that makes even this dour Swede's heart swell with joy.

2 Timothy 4:1–8
Psalm 71:8–9,14–15ab,16–17,22
Luke 2:41–51

*For this momentary light affliction is producing for us an eternal weight
of glory beyond all comparison, as we look not to what is seen but to
what is unseen; for what is seen is transitory, but what is unseen
is eternal.*

—2 CORINTHIANS 4:17–18

C. S. Lewis once gave a sermon at the University Church of
St. Mary the Virgin in Oxford, England, titled "The Weight
of Glory." It is now considered one of the most insightful
sermons of the twentieth century. In it, he contemplates the
meaning of the word *glory*. Glory can mean "fame" or
"luminosity," and many theologians define glory in this
context of fame—not as fame among people, but with God. I
suspect all the suffering we endure here on earth will fade
away into a distant memory when we hear the words "Well
done, my good and faithful servant." (NAB Matthew 25:21)

Genesis 3:9–15
Psalm 130:1–2,3–4,5–6,7–8
2 Corinthians 4:13—5:1
Mark 3:20–35

"Blessed are the poor in spirit,
for theirs is the Kingdom of heaven."
—MATTHEW 5:3

We often misread this verse as saying "Blessed are the poor"
instead of "Blessed are the poor *in spirit.*" But they go hand in
hand. Spiritual poverty describes a stance of utter
dependence on God, and that's easier to do when you're
poor. The rich don't need to depend on God—they can buy
their way out of problems. The writer Kathleen Norris once
said in a sermon, "When we think of ourselves as
self-sufficient in our riches, we are truly poor. Our lives
wither away, and in our desperation for control, we stunt the
lives of others, even those closest to us. . . . But when we
come to know ourselves as we really are: weak and
unfortunate creatures who need the love of God and other
people, it is then that we are rich."

Acts 11:21b–26; 13:1–3
Psalm 98:1,2–3ab,3cd–4,5–6
Matthew 5:1–12

JUNE 12

"Your light must shine before others, that they may see your good deeds and glorify your heavenly Father."
—MATTHEW 5:16

A few months ago, a friend at work asked to grab coffee with me. She was struggling with depression and told me she wanted to know more about my faith and my belief in God. I felt honored that she confided in me, but I felt completely ill-suited to give her any comfort or advice. I didn't want to offer any platitudes or try to convince her to believe in God. But the longer I am a Christian, the more I realize that we are not called to convince others to believe but to walk beside them and listen and help light the path as they begin their own journey toward God.

1 Kings 17:7–16
Psalm 4:2–3,4–5,7b–8
Matthew 5:13–16

Wednesday

JUNE 13

• ST. ANTHONY OF PADUA, PRIEST AND DOCTOR OF THE CHURCH •

"Answer me, LORD! Answer me, that this people may know that you,
LORD, are God and that you have brought them back from their senses."
The LORD'S fire came down and consumed the burnt offering, wood,
stones, and dust, and it lapped up the water in the trench. Seeing this, all
the people fell prostrate and said, "The LORD is God!
The LORD is God!"
—1 KINGS 18:37–39

There are times in our lives when we are suddenly shocked
out of our stupor. Maybe it's when we fall head-over-heels in
love. Or when someone close to us dies. Or when we lose a
job. Or when we see our first child being born. Our
pain—and our joy—often shakes us from our complacency
and lets us know the Lord is God. And we fall before
him in awe.

1 Kings 18:20–39
Psalm 16:1b–2ab,4,5ab and 8,11
Matthew 5:17–19

Thursday

JUNE 14

"If you bring your gift to the altar, and there recall that your brother has anything against you, leave your gift there at the altar, go first and be reconciled with your brother, and then come and offer your gift."
—MATTHEW 5:23–24

We may know of someone who has sin in his or her life but goes on ministering to others as though nothing is wrong. Or maybe we have been there ourselves—we don't want to acknowledge our sin and instead try to cover it up by acting more righteous and godly. But we can't fool God. In this Scripture he is saying, don't, just don't. Don't pretend to offer me your gifts when you're sinning against your brother (or sister). Go and confess, and repent, and pay the price. Make things right before you offer me your gifts.

1 Kings 18:41–46
Psalm 65:10,11,12–13
Matthew 5:20–26

Friday

JUNE 15

After the earthquake there was fire—but the LORD was not in the fire.
After the fire there was a tiny whispering sound. When he heard this,
Elijah hid his face in his cloak.
—1 KINGS 19:12

We expect God to come in an earthquake or a fire,
something dramatic and powerful. But sometimes he comes
in a whisper. The problem is that we are too busy, too
distracted, too self-absorbed to hear his voice. Are you being
still enough to hear his whispers?

1 Kings 19:9a,11–16
Psalm 27:7–8a,8b–9abc,13–14
Matthew 5:27–32

⇒ 195 ⇐

"Let your 'Yes' mean 'Yes,' and your 'No' mean 'No.' Anything more is from the Evil One."
—MATTHEW 5:37

When I was single, I tried to see every date and relationship as an opportunity to grow. One thing I learned was how to gracefully say no. It was hard, at first, when I knew a relationship wasn't working out, to let the guy down. I would hem and haw, beat around the bush, avoid the conversation. But in reality, I was just stringing the poor guy along and it ended up being more hurtful. And it was hurtful when one of my dates did the same thing to me. Jesus wants us to have the courage to be honest. Not to beat around the bush or try to explain so that it softens the blow but to have the integrity to say what we mean and mean what we say.

1 Kings 19:19–21
Psalm 16:1b–2a and 5,7–8,9–10
Matthew 5:33–37

Sunday

JUNE 17

• ELEVENTH SUNDAY IN ORDINARY TIME •

*We are always courageous, although we know that while we are at home
in the body we are away from the Lord.*
—2 CORINTHIANS 5:6

I grew up in Iowa but have lived in Chicago for several years.
Both places are my home. When I visit Iowa, I often feel
nostalgic for the wide-open spaces, my family who still lives
there, the sunsets, and the kind people. My husband and I
often talk of moving. But then when we return to Chicago,
we see the skyline and Lake Michigan and think of our
friends and our church here, and we know we can never leave
the city. So it is with Christians: Our home is here on earth
in our mortal bodies, but we also long for our eternal
home—when we will be with Christ.

Ezekiel 17:22–24
Psalm 92:2–3,13–14,15–16
2 Corinthians 5:6–10
Mark 4:26–34

Jesus said to his disciples: "You have heard that it was said, An eye for an eye and a tooth for a tooth. But I say to you, offer no resistance to one who is evil. When someone strikes you on your right cheek, turn the other one to him as well."

—MATTHEW 5:38–39

Is Jesus asking us to accept abuse at the hands of those who are evil in this passage? Surely not. This isn't about accepting and welcoming abuse from evil people. It's about not stooping to their level. If we seek revenge, then we are participating in the cycle of darkness. But if we "kill them with kindness," we are living in the light. We are called to say, "You have no power over me. I answer to a higher power and violence is not the answer."

1 Kings 21:1–16
Psalm 5:2–3ab,4b–6a,6b–7
Matthew 5:38–42

Tuesday

JUNE 19

• ST. ROMUALD, ABBOT •

*Jesus said to his disciples, "You have heard that it was said, 'You shall
love your neighbor and hate your enemy.' But I say to you, love
your enemies, and pray for those who persecute you . . . And if you greet
your brothers and sisters only, what is unusual about that? Do not the
pagans do the same?"*
—MATTHEW 5:43–44,47

When Jesus enters our world, he turns so many things upside
down. He helps us see everything in a new way: The first
shall be last; blessed are the poor; and in today's Scripture,
our enemies need love too. He points out that God loves
them, for he makes the sun rise on both the good and the
bad. In Christ's kingdom, we are called to be a light in the
darkness. To love the most unlovable—even our enemies.

1 Kings 21:17–29
Psalm 51:3–4,5–6ab,11 and 16
Matthew 5:43–48

JUNE 20

"Take care not to perform righteous deeds in order that people may see them; otherwise, you will have no recompense from your heavenly Father."
—MATTHEW 6:1

In the age of Facebook, Twitter, and Instagram, many of us feel compelled to document every little thing in our lives for all to see. Did your barista make an exceptionally pretty design in your latte? Post it on Instagram! Did your kid say something funny at dinner? Put it on Facebook! In this passage, Jesus says that what we do when no one is watching is more important. Even when you think no one is watching, and if your actions feel insignificant because you didn't post them on Facebook, know that God thinks what you do in private is significant and important, and that he will repay you.

2 Kings 2:1,6–14
Psalm 31:20,21,24
Matthew 6:1–6,16–18

Thursday

JUNE 21

> *"Our Father who art in heaven,*
> *hallowed be thy name,*
> *thy Kingdom come,*
> *thy will be done,*
> *on earth as it is in heaven."*
> —MATTHEW 6:9–10

Do not babble like the pagans, Jesus says in today's reading. Do not be like them, because your Father knows what you need before you ask him. Instead, pray "Thy Kingdom come, thy will be done . . ." This prayer reminds us, every week when we say it in Mass, that we can give up our need to control. God will give us what we need. How hard it is to say, "Thy will be done." But it's also a relief.

Sirach 48:1–14
Psalm 97:1–2,3–4,5–6,7
Matthew 6:7–15

Friday

JUNE 22

• ST. PAULINUS OF NOLA, BISHOP • SS. JOHN FISHER, BISHOP,
AND THOMAS MORE, MARTYRS •

*"Do not store up for yourselves treasures on earth, . . . But store up
treasures in heaven, . . . For where your treasure is, there also will
your heart be."*
—MATTHEW 6:19–21

Four months after my mom died suddenly of a heart attack
when she was only sixty-three years old, my father, siblings,
and I sorted through her belongings and had to decide what
to do with them. It was a difficult task—touching the fabric
of a blouse she had worn—and oddly absurd to think that
my mom was gone, but this insignificant blouse, shoes,
earrings, and perfume were still here with us. Ever since then,
I've viewed my "stuff" differently. The stuff we accumulate is
not what's important. What's important is finding our
significance in things that are much more eternal.

2 Kings 11:1–4,9–18,20
Psalm 132:11,12,13–14,17–18
Matthew 6:19–23

Saturday

JUNE 23

"Do not worry about tomorrow; tomorrow will take care of itself."
—MATTHEW 6:34

When I worry, my husband, who is a psychotherapist who
specializes in helping people with addictions, always reminds
me of the Alcoholics Anonymous mantra: "Take it one day at
a time." As a "big picture" person, I have a unique ability to
find things to worry about six months or a year from now.
But the Alcoholics Anonymous mantra reflects Jesus' words:
do not worry about tomorrow, or next month, or next year.
Only think about today, he says, and trust me.

2 Chronicles 24:17–25
Psalm 89:4–5,29–30,31–32,33–34
Matthew 6:24–34

To whomever I send you, you shall go;
whatever I command you, you shall speak.
Have no fear before them,
because I am with you to deliver you, says the LORD.
—JEREMIAH 1:7–8

In his book *Let Your Life Speak: Listening for the Voice of Vocation*, author Parker Palmer writes, "Our deepest calling is to grow into our own authentic self-hood, whether or not it conforms to some image of who we ought to be. As we do so, we will not only find the joy that every human being seeks—we will also find our path of authentic service in the world." God may call us to a place and to service that we least expect. But we can rest assured that wherever God calls us and whomever God calls us to become, he will give us the resources and courage to fulfill our calling.

VIGIL:
Jeremiah 1:4–10
Psalm 71:1–2,3–4a,5–6ab,15ab and 17
1 Peter 1:8–12
Luke 1:5–17

DAY:
Isaiah 49:1–6
Psalm 139:1b–3,13–14ab,14c–15
Acts 13:22–26
Luke 1:57–66,80

JUNE 25

"Why do you notice the splinter in your brother's eye, but do not perceive the wooden beam in your own eye?"
—MATTHEW 7:3

Jesus has a sense of humor. I laugh every time I read this passage and imagine a disciple with a huge wooden plank protruding from his eye. But it hits home, doesn't it? It's much easier for me to point out all of the little things my husband does wrong and much harder for me to swallow my pride and admit to my own wrongdoings. But only when we humble ourselves and remove our own "planks" can we effectively serve others.

2 Kings 17:5–8,13–15a,18
Psalm 60:3,4–5,12–13
Matthew 7:1–5

"Enter through the narrow gate; for the gate is wide and the road broad that leads to destruction, and those who enter through it are many. How narrow the gate and constricted the road that leads to life. And those who find it are few."

—MATTHEW 7:13–14

How hard it is to choose life. It's much easier to choose the easy way—those temporary things that bring momentary happiness but not lasting fulfillment or purpose. Will I cop out and surf the Internet for an hour, or will I be still and seek God? Will I go shopping over my lunch hour, or will I reach out to a hurting friend and ask her to lunch? Will I give up my comfortable life to follow Christ and do something risky but life-giving? I must choose daily to follow Christ—and enter the narrow gate that leads to life.

2 Kings 19:9b–11,14–21,31–35a,36
Psalm 48:2–3ab,3cd–4,10–11
Matthew 7:6,12–14

Lead me in the path of your commands,
for in it I delight.
Incline my heart to your decrees
and not to gain.
Turn away my eyes from seeing what is vain:
by your way give me life.
—PSALM 119:35–37

In the year following our foster daughter's placement with us, we kept a regular schedule and created routines and rituals. Our daughter needed boundaries in order to thrive, a container to work out her grief, and a safe place to feel what she needed to feel. It's not just hurting children who need structure. What at first might seem like stifling limitations can actually be a path to freedom. Poets work within structure. Writers have a word count they need to stay within. So, too, can we thrive in our spiritual lives by keeping God's commandments. God knows what we need to grow. We just need to trust and obey him.

2 Kings 22:8–13; 23:1–3
Psalm 119:33,34,36,37,40
Matthew 7:15–20

"Everyone who listens to these words of mine and acts on them will be like a wise man who built his house on a rock."
—MATTHEW 7:24

Desta watches a show called *Peg and Cat* on PBS. Peg and Cat use math to solve big problems. But Peg often feels overwhelmed and says, "I'm totally freaking out!" I can relate—I often freak out during difficult times. That's why I'm fascinated with the word *steadfast*. Psalm 112:6–7 says, "He shall not fear an ill report; / his heart is steadfast, trusting the LORD." The wise man is steadfast, building his house on a rock so no storms can wash it away. May I be like the wise man, steadfast and true, and not like Peg, freaking out over every trial that comes my way.

2 Kings 24:8–17
Psalm 79:1b–2,3–5,8,9
Matthew 7:21–29

Friday

JUNE 29

• SS. PETER AND PAUL, APOSTLES •

I, Paul, am already being poured out like a libation, and the time of my departure is at hand. I have competed well; I have finished the race; I have kept the faith.
—2 TIMOTHY 4:6–7

The act of pouring a libation was central to the Greek religion. A combination of water and wine, honey, oil, or milk was poured out as an offering to Zeus and the Olympian gods. Wine was also poured on animals before a ritual slaughter. Paul is saying that he has poured out his life as an offering to God. He has given everything. He has finished the race and competed well. He has kept the faith, and a crown of righteousness awaits him. At the end of our lives, let us hope that we too will feel like we have given everything to God. To hear God say, "Well done, good and faithful servant."

VIGIL:	DAY:
Acts 3:1–10	Acts 12:1–11
Psalm 19:2–3,4–5	Psalm 34:2–3,4–5,6–7,8–9
Galatians 1:11–20	2 Timothy 4:6–8,17–18
John 21:15–19	Matthew 16:13–19

*Pour out your heart like water
in the presence of the Lord.*
—LAMENTATIONS 2:19

When we first became foster parents to Desta, her former
foster family told us that when she was sad or angry, she
wailed so loudly and dramatically that it was as if she was
lamenting all the wrongs done to her black ancestors over
the past two centuries. We quickly learned this was
true—I've never seen a child cry so impressively. God wants
us to wail to him in our sadness, anger, frustration, and
disappointments. He can take it. He already knows our
hearts, anyway, and he wants to be with us in our laments.

Lamentations 2:2,10–14,18–19
Psalm 74:1b–2,3–5,6–7,20–21
Matthew 8:5–17

Sunday

JULY 1

• THIRTEENTH SUNDAY IN ORDINARY TIME •

For God formed man to be imperishable;
the image of his own nature he made him.
But by the envy of the devil, death entered the world,
and they who belong to his company experience it.
—WISDOM 2:23–24

Envy is one of the sins I struggle with the most. This
Scripture reminds us that because of the devil's envy, death
entered the world. That's how destructive envy can be.
When I feel envy toward those around me, I get obsessed
with what they have and what I don't have. My spirit dies a
little. My relationships suffer. My creativity dies. I am no
longer free. Hang out with the devil, and you will surely die.
Not physically, but spiritually.

Wisdom 1:13–15; 2:23–24
Psalm 30:2,4,5–6,11,12,13 (2a)
2 Corinthians 8:7,9,13–15
Mark 5:21–43 or 5:21–24, 35b–43

"Lord, let me go first and bury my father." But Jesus answered him,
"Follow me, and let the dead bury their dead."
—MATTHEW 8:21–22

Throughout Scripture, Jesus asks his followers to leave things
behind: their possessions, their families, even their dead
loved ones. It seems a bit harsh, not allowing the disciple to
go to his father's funeral. But I think what Jesus is getting at
here is that when he says "Follow me," we can't hesitate,
wondering what business we need to take care of before we
follow. We have to be willing to let go of our own agenda.

Amos 2:6–10,13–16
Psalm 50:16bc–17,18–19,20–21,22–23
Matthew 8:18–22

But Thomas said to them, "Unless I see the mark of the nails in his hands and put my finger into the nailmarks and put my hand into his side, I will not believe."
—JOHN 20:25

Oh, doubting Thomas. He gets a bad rap, but I can relate to him. I have learned, though, that doubt is an essential part of faith. The opposite of faith isn't doubt; it's certainty. Frederick Buechner writes in *Wishful Thinking*, "Whether your faith is that there is a God or that there is not a God, if you don't have any doubts you are either kidding yourself or asleep. Doubts are the ants in the pants of faith. They keep it awake and moving."

Ephesians 2:19–22
Psalm 117:1bc,2
John 20:24–29

Wednesday

JULY 4

• INDEPENDENCE DAY •

For mine are all the animals of the forests,
beasts by the thousands on my mountains.
I know all the birds of the air,
and whatever stirs in the plains, belongs to me.
—PSALM 50:10–11

There used to be 75 million buffalo roaming the plains of the United States. Explorers Lewis and Clark described them as "the moving multitude that darkened the whole plains" when they encountered them at South Dakota's White River in 1806. But by 1830, systematic reduction of herds began as America expanded westward. Sport hunters often killed up to 250 per day, and by 1883 the herds were destroyed, with only 300 wild buffalo remaining in the United States and Canada. Today we are losing animals throughout the world to poaching or loss of habitat. God says the animals are his. Why aren't we doing more to protect that which has been entrusted to us?

Amos 5:14–15,21–24
Psalm 50:7,8–9,10–11,12–13,16bc–17
Matthew 8:28–34

The fear of the LORD is pure, enduring forever.
—PSALM 19:10

What does it mean to fear the Lord? We often think of this as fear of being punished. But in this context, the meaning is more nuanced. There's a difference between "servile fear" (fear of getting in trouble) and "filial fear" (fear of offending someone we love). In *The Problem of Pain*, Anglican writer C. S. Lewis explained that fear of the Lord is not a fear that one feels for a tiger or even a ghost. Rather, it is the experience of being filled with awe, in which you "feel wonder and a certain shrinking" or "a sense of inadequacy to cope with such a visitant of or prostration before it." May we stand before the Lord, not shaking in our shoes with fear, but lying prostrate before him in awe.

Amos 7:10–17
Psalm 19:8,9,10,11
Matthew 9:1–8

• ST. MARIA GORETTI, VIRGIN AND MARTYR •

"I did not come to call the righteous but sinners."
—MATTHEW 9:13

Jesus hung out with tax collectors, prostitutes, adulterers, and other types of obvious sinners. This confounded the Pharisees to no end. But they were, in fact, sinners too; they just didn't acknowledge it. They thought they were doing okay because they were keeping all the rules. When we think we're doing okay, we don't think we need to ask for help. The Pharisees needed as much help as any sinner, but because they didn't realize that, Jesus could not help them.

Amos 8:4–6,9–12
Psalm 119:2,10,20,30,40,131
Matthew 9:9–13

Kindness and truth shall meet;
justice and peace shall kiss.
Truth shall spring out of the earth,
and justice shall look down from heaven.
—PSALM 85:11–12

While writing this book, I woke one morning to read about
two more black men who had been killed by police officers.
One man was killed in Louisiana, the other in Minnesota.
One was selling CDs in a parking lot, the other was driving a
car with a broken taillight. How many black men will perish
without justice being served? I want to believe in the justice
of God, but on some days it's nearly impossible to imagine
any kind of justice for the black lives that have been taken
throughout the history of our country. Come, Lord Jesus.

Amos 9:11–15
Psalm 85:9ab and 10,11–12,13–14
Matthew 9:14–17

"My grace is sufficient for you, for power is made perfect in weakness."
—2 CORINTHIANS 12:9

I once had a boss who told me I was too "weak." He saw me this way because I didn't speak up in meetings and wasn't competitive enough. For a while, I tried to become someone I was not: an extroverted, competitive, talkative, type-A person. But while I may have changed the perception that I was weak, my soul was slowly dying. I finally realized that I didn't want to be the person my boss was asking me to be. I liked that God made me quiet and contemplative. I wanted to value compassion over competition. I didn't want to pretend that I was perfect all the time. I realized that there is power in what our society often believes is weakness. And God can work through us.

Ezekiel 2:2–5
Psalm 123:1–2,2,3–4
2 Corinthians 12:7–10
Mark 6:1–6

• ST. AUGUSTINE ZHAO RONG, PRIEST, AND COMPANIONS, MARTYRS •

Every day I will bless you,
and I will praise your name forever and ever.
—PSALM 145:2

Often, Lord, I wake up in the morning and get on with my day without giving you a second thought. I have urgent things to do. I eat breakfast, check social media, take my daughter to school, go to work, come home and make dinner, watch TV. But sometimes I stop and realize your grace and mercy in my life, and I praise you. Forgive me for not doing it every day.

Hosea 2:16,17b–18,21–22
Psalm 145:2–3,4–5,6–7,8–9
Matthew 9:18–26

*At the sight of the crowds, his heart was moved with pity for them
because they were troubled and abandoned, like sheep without a shepherd.
Then he said to his disciples, "The harvest is abundant but the laborers
are few; so ask the master of the harvest to send out laborers for
his harvest."*
—MATTHEW 9:36–38

How many times are we moved by the souls around us who
are troubled and abandoned? Too many times we ignore
them because we don't have time, or we have too much
going on. But to be disciples of Christ means we are called to
be laborers in the harvest. We are called to give hope to
those who need it most.

Hosea 8:4–7,11–13
Psalm 115:3–4,5–6,7ab–8,9–10
Matthew 9:32–38

Wednesday

JULY 11

• ST. BENEDICT, ABBOT •

Look to the LORD in his strength;
seek to serve him constantly.
Recall the wondrous deeds that he has wrought.
—PSALM 105:4–5

When I was going through unemployment, infertility, and
the seeming death of all my dreams, a friend suggested,
"Have you ever tried a gratitude journal?" This sounded to
me like the equivalent of putting a bandage on a cancer
patient. And yet I've been wondering if it could help to look
back and see how God might be putting together all the
pieces. Maybe keeping a list of things you are thankful for is
just a reminder that God's grace is new every morning. That
God is lurking in the middle of the mess, showing up in ways
you may never expect. Maybe the beauty of gratitude
journals is simply helping us see.

Hosea 10:1–3,7–8,12
Psalm 105:2–3,4–5,6–7
Matthew 10:1–7

*"As you go, make this proclamation: 'The Kingdom of Heaven
is at hand.'"*
—MATTHEW 10:7

My daughter has a book titled *Fancy Nancy: The Backwards
Day!* by Jane O'Connor. In the story, it's Backwards Day at
Nancy's school, where everyone wears their clothes
backwards and says the opposite of what they mean. Now
Desta tells me, "Mommy, I hate you!" and then she laughs
because she really means, "Mommy, I love you!" The
kingdom of heaven is like Backwards Day: the first shall be
last, the sick will be healed, the dead will be raised. We go
through life thinking that success comes from making lots of
money, but sometimes success happens in poverty.
Sometimes you have to get sick to be spiritually healed, and
those who are the most vulnerable have the most courage.
We are called to spread the Good News about this crazy,
upside down, backwards-day kingdom.

Hosea 11:1–4,8e–9
Psalm 80:2ac and 3b,15–16
Matthew 10:7–15

Friday

JULY 13

• ST. HENRY •

"You will be hated by all because of my name, but whoever endures to the end will be saved."
—MATTHEW 10:22

Every summer there's a 468-mile bike ride across Iowa, that starts at the Missouri River and ends at the Mississippi River. A few years ago, all my siblings rode it, and I lamented to my sister that my work schedule didn't allow me to join them. She told me later that while it was gratifying to finish the long seven-day ride, it was also grueling. "Some days," she told me, "I had to tell myself 'Just keep pedaling! Just keep pedaling!'" Sometimes faith looks like endurance. On days when you are overwhelmed, exhausted, discouraged, when you think you can't go on but you get up and face another day anyway, you are being faithful. God knows, understands, and honors you for it. Just keep pedaling.

Hosea 14:2–10
Psalm 51:3–4,8–9,12–13,14 and 17
Matthew 10:16–23

Saturday

JULY 14

• ST. KATERI TEKAKWITHA, VIRGIN •

Then I heard the voice of the LORD saying, "Whom shall I send? Who will go for us?" "Here I am," I said; "send me!"
—ISAIAH 6:8

When God asks us to do his work, are we willing? Do we answer quickly and eagerly? Or do we hesitate, find excuses, and shrink back because we are afraid or too busy? God wants to use us—we just need to be available and willing.

Isaiah 6:1–8
Psalm 93:1ab,1cd–2,5
Matthew 10:24–33

*In him we were also chosen, destined in accord with the purpose of the
One who accomplishes all things.*
—EPHESIANS 1:11

There's something wonderful about being chosen. Whether
we're getting picked first for the kickball team in elementary
school or we're being chosen by someone to marry, it affirms
our self-worth and the fact that we are lovable. By contrast,
not being chosen feels horrible. I have many single friends
who feel that something is wrong with them because they
have not been "chosen." I mourn for them. God says we are
chosen by him. If only we could understand this and
remember it every time we don't feel valued and loved.

Amos 7:12–15
Psalm 85:9–10,11–12,13–14 (8)
Ephesians 1:3–14 or 1:3–10
Mark 6:7–13

"Whoever loves father or mother more than me is not worthy of me, and whoever loves son or daughter more than me is not worthy of me."
—MATTHEW 10:37

I still remember the looks on my parents' faces as I drove out of the driveway. My Ford Escort was stuffed with my possessions. I had finished a master's degree in journalism while living with my parents for three years, and now it was time for me to move to Chicago to pursue my calling. I was finally leaving home, and the pain on their faces slayed me. I didn't want to disappoint them: my dad wanted me to stay in Iowa and find a job there. But I knew I needed to leave. Sometimes it's hard to follow God to places where others may not understand.

Isaiah 1:10–17
Psalm 50:8–9,16bc–17,21 and 23
Matthew 10:34—11:1

*Great is the LORD and wholly to be praised
in the city of our God.
His holy mountain, fairest of heights,
is the joy of all the earth.*
—PSALM 48:2–3A

The highlight of summer when I was a teen was church camp. The weeks were filled with speakers, workshops, Bible studies—and also fun, of course. For young Baptist teens, it could be spiritually exhilarating—a mountaintop experience—and we all came home from camp with a renewed commitment to follow Jesus. Inevitably, we had to deal with real life, but I'm sure we were forever changed in some small way. Bible commentator William Barclay says, "The moment of glory does not exist for its own sake; it exists to clothe the common things with a radiance they never had before." Praise God for his holy mountain, the joy of all the earth.

Isaiah 7:1–9
Psalm 48:2–3a,3b–4,5–6,7–8
Matthew 11:20–24

For the LORD will not cast off his people.
—PSALM 94:14

St. Camillus de Lellis, an excessive gambler who as a child was neglected by his family, was constantly plagued by a leg wound he received while in the army that failed to heal. While being treated in a hospital that cared for those with incurable diseases, he saw how poorly the patients were treated and felt called to dedicate his life to caring for the sick. Camillus was beatified by Pope Benedict XIV in 1742 and canonized four years later. I heard someone say once that there's a difference between being cured and being healed. Sometimes our wounds are never cured, but it's because of them our souls are healed. Praise be to God.

Isaiah 10:5–7,13b–16
Psalm 94:5–6,7–8,9–10,14–15
Matthew 11:25–27

Thursday
JULY 19

*"Come to me, all you who labor and are burdened, and I will give
you rest."*
—MATTHEW 11:28

Since becoming a parent, I have experienced nonstop
exhaustion. The combination of working full time,
completing writing projects on the side, and caring for a now
six-year-old has left me depleted. These words are a balm to
my soul. If only I would remember to rest in God, to
surrender my worries and anxiety, my hurried, stress-filled
days. Why don't I respond to his invitation more often?

Isaiah 26:7–9,12,16–19
Psalm 102:13–14ab and 15,16–18,19–21
Matthew 11:28–30

⇒ 229 ⇐

*"I say to you, something greater than the temple is here. If you knew
what this meant, I desire mercy, not sacrifice."*
—MATTHEW 12:6–7

Laws have their place. Without them, we'd have anarchy. But
laws also have limits. In today's Scripture, the Pharisees saw
the disciples walking through a field on the Sabbath, eating
the heads of grain. They said to Jesus, "See, your disciples are
doing what is unlawful to do on the Sabbath." Jesus told
them that there was something better than the law. Laws can
be oppressive, demeaning, and ostracizing. Jesus came to
offer something more life-giving. You cannot legalize
compassion, forgiveness, communion, or love.

Isaiah 38:1–6,21–22,7–8
Isaiah 38:10,11,12abcd,16
Matthew 12:1–8

Saturday

JULY 21

• ST. LAWRENCE OF BRINDISI, PRIEST AND DOCTOR OF THE CHURCH •

Why, O LORD, do you stand aloof?
Why hide in times of distress?
—PSALM 10:1

A few years ago, during a stretch of unemployment,
infertility, and a failed adoption, I gave God a new name:
"Ghost God." In my pain, I could not feel his presence, figure
out what he was doing in my life, or understand what the
purpose was for all this pain. "Where are you, God?! What is
the meaning of all this? And do you even exist?" In some
ways, it's comforting to know that the psalmist experienced
Ghost God as well. Apparently, he has been hiding from his
followers for ages. Funny thing is, he tends to show up when
you least expect it. Sometimes you can catch a glimpse of
him lurking in the shadows. At other times his presence is as
real as if he were standing two feet away, and I can feel his
warm breath on my face.

Micah 2:1–5
Psalm 10:1–2,3–4,7–8,14
Matthew 12:14–21

When he disembarked and saw the vast crowd, his heart was moved with pity for them.
—MARK 6:34

They were tired. All Jesus and the disciples wanted to do was go off to a deserted place to rest. But the crowd caught wind of where they were going and followed them. Any parent knows how this feels; you try to find someplace in your home where you can be alone and decompress, but your children always know where to find you, and they appear before you've had time to take a deep breath. We love our children but need our own time too. Jesus sacrificed his own needs for that of the crowd, who were like lost sheep. Sometimes we must defer our needs if we are to love others.

Jeremiah 23:1–6
Psalm 23:1–3,3–4,5,6 (1)
Ephesians 2:13–18
Mark 6:30–34

Monday

JULY 23

• ST. BRIDGET, RELIGIOUS •

With what shall I come before the LORD,
and bow before God most high?
Shall I come before him with burnt offerings,
with calves a year old? . . .
You have been told, O man, what is good,
and what the LORD requires of you:
Only to do the right and to love goodness,
and to walk humbly with your God.
—MICAH 6:6,8

God doesn't want our offerings or sacrifices. It's not about what we can do for God but who we are becoming and how we are being transformed. Transformation is the harder path, to be sure. It's easy to bring a peace offering but much more difficult to open ourselves to God, who will change us from the inside out. Or to be gutted by the suffering that comes our way and to let it change us. This willingness for transformation is part of what it means to walk humbly with God.

Micah 6:1–4,6–8
Psalm 50:5–6,8–9,16bc–17,21 and 23
Matthew 12:38–42

You will cast into the depths of the sea all our sins.
—MICAH 7:19

Challenger Deep, the deepest part of the ocean, is 36,200 feet deep. That's almost seven miles. Any part of the ocean deeper than 3.7 miles is called the "hadal zone." The term *hadal* comes from "Hades"—the Greek god of the underworld—but it can also mean "abode of the dead." In Greek mythology, Hades strictly prevented inhabitants of his dominion from leaving. In hadal zones, species are often incapable of leaving the deep trenches of the sea bottom. Take comfort knowing that your sins have been cast into the hadal zones of the ocean. They are miles below the surface, confined to the deep trenches for all eternity. Don't try to dredge them up.

Micah 7:14–15,18–20
Psalm 85:2–4,5–6,7–8
Matthew 12:46–50

Wednesday

JULY 25

• ST. JAMES, APOSTLE •

*We too believe and therefore speak, knowing that the one who raised the
Lord Jesus will raise us also with Jesus and place us with you in
his presence.*
—2 CORINTHIANS 4:14–15

I once asked my daughter what superpower she would
choose if she could have one. She said it would be to be
invisible. A handy superpower, indeed, if you're a
mischievous six-year-old. But most of us do not want to be
invisible. We want to be seen and understood. I often feel
invisible at work or at home, and I give up trying to explain
myself because it takes too much effort. But God knows me.
Even before I was in my mother's womb, God knew me. He's
raised me and placed me in his presence. When you feel
alone and invisible, rest in the One who has known you even
before you were a zygote.

2 Corinthians 4:7–15
Psalm 126:1bc–2ab,2cd–3,4–5,6
Matthew 20:20–28

JULY 26

• SS. JOACHIM AND ANNE, PARENTS OF THE BLESSED VIRGIN MARY •

"This is why I speak to them in parables, because they look but do
not see and hear but do not listen or understand."
—MATTHEW 13:13

My philosophy professor once said that if we could
understand God, he wouldn't be a God worth serving. One
thing I like about the Catholic Church is that Catholics feel
comfortable with mystery. Mystics believe that spiritual
apprehension of truths is beyond the intellect. Thomas
Merton wrote in *New Seeds of Contemplation* that nothing could
be more alien to contemplation than the *cogito ergo sum* of
Descartes: "I think, therefore I am." Jesus knew that his
message was difficult for people to grasp. The closest he
could get to explaining it was through comparing the
kingdom to a mustard seed, to a treasure in a field, to a pearl.
These were pale comparisons, but they were a start.

Jeremiah 2:1–3,7–8,12–13
Psalm 36:6–7ab,8–9,10–11
Matthew 13:10–17

The seed sown on rich soil is the one who hears the word and understands it, who indeed bears fruit and yields a hundred or sixty or thirtyfold.
—MATTHEW 13:23

In the parable of the sower, Jesus describes many ways we hear the word of the kingdom: as the seed sown on the path (we can hear it and not understand it), as the seed sown on rocky ground (we can hear it and receive it joyfully—but immediately forget about it), and as the seed sown among thorns (we can hear it but then get distracted by everyday anxieties and ambitions). Or, we can hear the word of the kingdom as a seed sown on rich soil. Our souls must be soft, open, welcoming, and prepared for the roots to grow deep. It is in such a life that the seeds will bear much fruit.

Jeremiah 3:14–17
Jeremiah 31:10,11–12abcd,13
Matthew 13:18–23

Saturday

JULY 28

Only if you thoroughly reform your ways and your deeds; if each of you deals justly with his neighbor; if you no longer oppress the resident alien, the orphan, and the widow . . . will I remain with you in this place.
—JEREMIAH 7:5–7

Who can ever forget the image of a Syrian toddler lying facedown on the beach in Greece after drowning on his way to find refuge with his family? Refugees risk everything to escape war, persecution, torture. But more countries, including our own USA, are lessening or stopping altogether the flow of refugees across our borders. We hold onto another image, though: Greeks who stood on the shores of their country, welcoming the Syrian refugees, helping them out of their flimsy boats, carrying children to shore as parents wept with relief. They are doing the work of God.

Jeremiah 7:1–11
Psalm 84:3,4,5–6a and 8a,11
Matthew 13:24–30

⇒ 238 ⇐

*You open your hand
and satisfy the desire of every living thing.*
—PSALM 145:16

We often think our desires are bad or that there's something we must sacrifice to follow Christ. But God created us with desires, and we need to listen to them and allow God to work through them. Fr. James Martin, SJ, says that desire is a key way in which we hear God's voice. He writes, "The deep longings of our hearts are our holy desires. Not only desires for physical healing, but also the desires for change, for growth, for a fuller life. Our deepest desires, those desires that lead us to become who we are, are God's desires for us. They are ways that God speaks to you directly." What do you desire?

2 Kings 4:42–44
Psalm 145:10–11,15–16,17–18
Ephesians 4:1–6
John 6:1–15

"I will open my mouth in parables, I will announce what has
lain hidden from the foundation of the world."
—MATTHEW 13:35

Jesus says that the kingdom of heaven is like a mustard seed
that grows into a large bush where birds dwell. Or, the
kingdom of heaven is like yeast that a woman mixes with
flour until the whole batch is leavened. He also compares the
kingdom to a treasure in a field and then to a fine pearl. So, if
the kingdom is like a tiny seed, yeast, a treasure, and a fine
pearl, do we have any idea what it's like? Many times, Jesus'
parables left his followers puzzled. But from these verses we
can conclude that the kingdom may start small but grow into
something big and life-giving; it provides abundantly, and it's
beautiful. That sounds good to me.

Jeremiah 13:1–11
Deuteronomy 32:18–19,20,21
Matthew 13:31–35

Tuesday

JULY 31

• ST. IGNATIUS OF LOYOLA, PRIEST •

Among the nations' idols is there any that gives rain?
Or can the mere heavens send showers?
—JEREMIAH 14:22

It's easy to see idolatry in hindsight, or when other people do it. But when we're in the midst of worshipping idols—whatever they may be—we can't see how ridiculous our choices are. How can we give up worshipping the one true God so that we can give our lives to money or beauty or success or following our favorite sports team? Eventually, we realize that our idols can do nothing for us—not even send us rain.

Jeremiah 14:17–22
Psalm 79:8,9,11 and 13
Matthew 13:36–43

*Why is my pain continuous,
my wound incurable, refusing to be healed?*
—JEREMIAH 15:18

I started getting migraines when I was twenty-five. Often, I
would miss three days of work because I couldn't get out of
bed. In the middle of a migraine attack, I would become
desolate, feeling that the pain would never go away, that I
would never be well again. Fortunately, my doctor identified
the medication that could alleviate the pain. Some people
have chronic pain that cannot be cured. From what I
understand, it's not just the physical pain that's so bad—it's
also the isolation and loneliness. How long, oh Lord, we cry.
Please heal us from our afflictions. Or at least give us the
strength to endure.

Jeremiah 15:10,16–21
Psalm 59:2–3,4,10–11,17,18
Matthew 13:44–46

Thursday

AUGUST 2

• ST. EUSEBIUS OF VERCELLI, BISHOP • ST. PETER JULIAN EYMARD, PRIEST •

*Whenever the object of clay which he was making turned out badly in
his hand, he tried again, making of the clay another object of whatever
sort he pleased.*
—JEREMIAH 18:4

We are clay in the hands of the Potter. We can view this as
something negative and passive: we are not in control, we are
squeezed and pushed and molded into whatever God wants,
which may not feel comfortable. Or, we can see ourselves as
precious material from which God creates works of art. And
if something goes wrong, there's always a second chance
because the Potter can rework our lives and create something
beautiful.

Jeremiah 18:1–6
Psalm 146:1b–2,3–4,5–6ab
Matthew 13:47–53

———————

"Is he not the carpenter's son?"
—MATTHEW 13:55

Life in small towns changes slowly or hardly at all. Kids graduate from high school and stay put. The same small businesses plug along, year after year. The same floats and bands and Shriners show up in the Fourth of July parades. So, imagine if a son of a local carpenter, who had left town years ago, returned to town, performing miracles and claiming to be the Messiah. Of course people would be skeptical. Those in Jesus' hometown saw him for who he had been, not for who he had become. If he was the Messiah, what would it mean for their comfortable, safe existence? Unfortunately, their fears and prejudices would prevent their finding out.

Jeremiah 26:1–9
Psalm 69:5,8–10,14
Matthew 13:54–58

Let not the flood-waters overwhelm me.
—PSALM 69:16

Water can be treacherous and frightening. I will never forget watching footage of the 2004 earthquake and the resulting tsunami in the Indian Ocean, how people on the beach, unaware of the danger, were swept up in the wall of water. Where I live, Lake Michigan can be frightening when the winds blow the waves over Lake Shore Drive, a major highway into Chicago. Sometimes the road is closed because the waves are too high. But throughout Scripture, Jesus calms the storm, walks on water, or parts the sea. However frightening the water may be, Jesus is more powerful. Remember this today if you feel overwhelmed, as if you're sinking.

Jeremiah 26:11–16,24
Psalm 69:15–16,30–31,33–34
Matthew 14:1–12

AUGUST 5

• EIGHTEENTH SUNDAY IN ORDINARY TIME •

"I am the bread of life; whoever comes to me will never hunger, and whoever believes in me will never thirst."
—JOHN 6:35

Jesus transforms human hunger into God-hunger. In Scripture, he's constantly eating with the outcasts and strangers and sinners. And when he does, he turns the meal into a talk about spiritual hunger. He is the bread of life—that basic dietary staple that shows up in nearly every culture. But his type of bread will satisfy more than growling bellies. What are you hungry for?

Exodus 16:2–4,12–15
Psalm 78:3–4,23–24,25,54 (24b)
Ephesians 4:17,20–24
John 6:24–35

AUGUST 6

• THE TRANSFIGURATION OF THE LORD •

And he was transfigured before them, and his clothes became
dazzling white.
—MARK 9:3

Jesus took Peter, James, and John up to a mountaintop (some
believe this is Mt. Hermon), where he was transfigured
before them. Suddenly, the disciples saw a glimpse of Christ's
divinity and the merging of heaven and earth. A friend of
mine is dying of cancer. She is closer to heaven than most of
us understand. She is standing on Mt. Hermon, being
transformed. I can sense it in her spirit and in her writing. In
my grief over her illness, I am in awe of her brilliance. The
space between heaven and earth is narrow. In rare moments
like these—when a friend is dying or some miracle
happens—we see these "thin places." When I am burdened
by the evil and sadness in the world, I cling to these dazzling
white moments.

Daniel 7:9–10,13–14
Psalm 97:1–2,5–6,9
2 Peter 1:16–19
Mark 9:2–10

AUGUST 7

• ST. SIXTUS II, POPE, AND COMPANIONS, MARTYRS • ST. CAJETAN, PRIEST •

"Lord, save me!" Immediately Jesus stretched out his hand and caught him, and said to him, "O you of little faith, why did you doubt?"
—MATTHEW 14:30–31

Not long ago, my marriage was battered by the winds and waves. My husband and I felt like we were sinking. I didn't know if we could put it back together. We went to therapy and worked hard. I prayed. *Who can save us?* Someone reminded me that I was a person of faith. *Yes,* I said. And I clung to Christ's words to his disciples: "It is I; do not be afraid." And then, just a few weeks ago, I sat in our therapist's office and marveled at how far we had come. We had walked across the stormy sea and grabbed the hand of Christ. We could say, "Truly, you are the Son of God."

Jeremiah 30:1–2,12–15,18–22
Psalm 102:16–18,19–21,29 and 22–23
Matthew 14:22–36 or 15:1–2,10–14

Shouting, they shall mount the heights of Zion,
they shall come streaming to the LORD'S blessings.
Then the virgins shall make merry and dance,
and young men and old as well.
I will turn their mourning into joy.
I will console and gladden them after their sorrows.
—JEREMIAH 31:12–13

I remember driving by the high school during prom, looking in through the open gym doors at the kids dancing and having fun in their taffeta dresses and black tuxes. I was not allowed to attend because of certain religious beliefs, but the larger message I picked up in those days was that joy could be dangerous. I have spent the rest of my life fighting that feeling. Why is joy so scary and threatening? God, let me experience joy and gladness. Help me remember your blessings and dance with joy.

Jeremiah 31:1–7
Jeremiah 31:10,11–12ab,13
Matthew 15:21–28

"Get behind me, Satan! You are an obstacle to me. You are thinking not as God does but as human beings do."
—MATTHEW 16:23

Jesus has just told his disciples that he must go to Jerusalem and suffer greatly from the elders, chief priests, and scribes, and then be killed but rise on the third day. Peter takes him aside and says, "God forbid! No such thing shall ever happen to you!" Jesus replies by calling him Satan and an obstacle. That response sounds harsh, but Jesus could not be dissauded from his mission. He had the divine vision, and Peter's human agenda was getting in the way. Beware: Satan uses others, even seemingly well-meaning friends, to keep us from our mission, from being all God has created us to be.

Jeremiah 31:31–34
Psalm 51:12–13,14–15,18–19
Matthew 16:13–23

Each must do as already determined, without sadness or compulsion, for
God loves a cheerful giver.
—2 CORINTHIANS 9:7

Some of us are anxious givers, prying open our wallets
because we're worried about paying the bills. God gets
whatever is left over. A cheerful giver trusts God to provide.
The more I trust, the more I can let go of the security of my
bank account and give cheerfully to God and others.

2 Corinthians 9:6–10
Psalm 112:1–2,5–6,7–8,9
John 12:24–26

Saturday

AUGUST 11

• ST. CLARE, VIRGIN •

They trust in you who cherish your name,
for you forsake not those who seek you, O LORD.
—PSALM 9:11

St. Clare came from a wealthy family in Assisi, and when, at
the age of eighteen, she heard Francis of Assisi speak during
a Lenten service, she committed her life to God. On Palm
Sunday, 1212, she left home and went to the chapel of
Porziuncula to meet Francis, cut her hair, and exchange her
expensive clothes for a plain robe. Her father attempted to
force her to come home, but she clung to the altar of the
church. I love that image of her clinging to the altar, refusing
to go. What love and passion she had for God! On her
deathbed, she said, "Blessed be You, O God, for having
created me." I chose St. Clare as my patron saint when I
became Catholic—may I follow her example of clinging to
the altar for dear life.

Habakkuk 1:12—2:4
Psalm 9:8–9,10–11,12–13
Matthew 17:14–20

Elijah went a day's journey into the desert, until he came to a broom tree and sat beneath it. He prayed for death saying: "This is enough, O LORD!"
—1 KINGS 19:4

Have you ever wanted to give up? Have you ever been so weary that you felt you couldn't go on? Elijah, after praying for death, fell asleep. An angel touched him and ordered him to eat and drink. Then Elijah lay down again, and the angel ordered him to get up again and eat and drink. Strengthened by food and rest, he walked on forty more days and nights. Sometimes, when we are weary and can't go on, all we need is some rest, and some food, and some divine intervention, and we will find the strength to go on.

1 Kings 19:4–8
Psalm 34:2–3,4–5,6–7,8–9 (9a)
Ephesians 4:30—5:2
John 6:41–51

AUGUST 13

• SS. PONTIAN, POPE, AND HIPPOLYTUS, PRIEST, MARTYRS •

"The Son of Man is to be handed over to men, and they will kill him, and he will be raised on the third day." And they were overwhelmed with grief.
—MATTHEW 17:22–23

God created us with imaginations, and, when we imagine ourselves inside a Gospel story, God can speak to us personally. If we place ourselves inside today's story, we can imagine how confused and sad the disciples must have felt. They had given up everything to follow Christ, and now he told them he would be killed. I wonder if they felt betrayed, that they had made a huge mistake following this Jesus of Nazareth. They were too distraught to hear him when he said that he would be raised on the third day. Are you grieving today? Try to imagine the Resurrection on the other side of your grief.

Ezekiel 1:2–5,24–28c
Psalm 148:1–2,11–12,13,14
Matthew 17:22–27

Tuesday

AUGUST 14

• ST. MAXIMILIAN KOLBE, PRIEST AND MARTYR •

"Amen, I say to you, unless you turn and become like children, you will not enter the Kingdom of heaven."
—MATTHEW 18:3

My daughter has ADHD and has a hard time sitting still during Mass. She crawls under the pew, wiggles, and talks too loudly. For a while we didn't even take her. And yet I have always said that she's the spiritual leader in our family. Amid the whirlwind that is her life, she sometimes pauses and says things that surprise me. "Mommy, where is God?" she asked me one morning, which led to an interesting discussion: me trying to explain the presence of God to a four-year-old. Then, a few weeks ago during Mass, out of the blue she leaned over and whispered (a bit too loudly), "Mommy, God loves everyone!" I smiled at her. I hope she always finds comfort in knowing that God has her back.

Ezekiel 2:8—3:4
Psalm 119:14,24,72,103,111,131
Matthew 18:1–5,10,12–14

While Jesus was speaking, a woman from the crowd called out and said to him, "Blessed is the womb that carried you and the breasts at which you nursed." He replied, "Rather, blessed are those who hear the word of God and observe it."

—LUKE 11:27–28

This seems a bit harsh, doesn't it? Shouldn't Jesus have said something like, "Yes, blessed is the womb that carried me. Great is my mother among women!" Instead, he turned the conversation back onto the woman in the crowd. He didn't want his message to be about him, or his mother—no matter how wonderful she was. He wanted the crowd to understand that it was about *them* hearing the word of God and observing it. Throughout Scripture, Jesus reminds us to focus on the most important things.

VIGIL:	DAY:
1 Chronicles 15:3–4,15–16; 16:1–2	Revelation 11:19a; 12:1–6a,10ab
Psalm 132:6–7,9–10,13–14	Psalm 45:10,11,12,16
1 Corinthians 15:54b–57	1 Corinthians 15:20–27
Luke 11:27–28	Luke 1:39–56

Thursday

AUGUST 16

"Lord, if my brother sins against me, how often must I forgive him? As many as seven times?" Jesus answered, "I say to you, not seven times but seventy-seven times."
—MATTHEW 18:21–22

One of the top-grossing films of all time is *Love Story*, a 1970 film about college students who fall in love. Oliver comes from a rich family, and Jenny from a working-class family, so of course his parents do not approve. They marry anyway, and they live happily ever after, until (spoiler alert) Jenny gets leukemia and dies. A famous quote from the film is, "Love means never having to say you're sorry." Any married couple knows how absurd that is. Love means *always* having to say you're sorry—and having to forgive each other over and over again. Jesus tells us to forgive not just seven times but seventy-seven times. Maybe it doesn't make a great movie quote, but that's what true love is.

Ezekiel 12:1–12
Psalm 78:56–57,58–59,61–62
Matthew 18:21—19:1

AUGUST 17

But you were captivated by your own beauty, you used your renown to make yourself a harlot.

—EZEKIEL 16:15

Ezekiel compares Israel to a beautiful harlot. God bestowed upon her beauty and adorned her with gold and silver, and yet she turned around and used those gifts for evil. The best part of this passage is that God still pardons her for all she has done. We sometimes become obsessed with the gifts God has given us and use them for our own glory. What gifts have I used for evil? And do I really know—to the depth of my bones—that I am pardoned?

Ezekiel 16:1–15,60,63 or 16:59–63
Isaiah 12:2–3,4bcd,5–6
Matthew 19:3–12

"Let the children come to me, and do not prevent them; for the Kingdom of heaven belongs to such as these."
—MATTHEW 19:14

One Sunday, to my horror, the nursery at our church was closed. I had taken Desta to church by myself because David was out of town. I had to decide whether to go home or take her with me to Mass. "Take me to the Big Church!" Desta pleaded. Against my better judgment, I did. Surprisingly, she sat peacefully on my lap the whole time. She sang "Glories to God in the highest!" as loudly as she could. When it came time for the Eucharist, she whispered loudly, "Mommy, I want some! I want some!" The priest smiled as he made the sign of the cross on her forehead and blessed her. Jesus said unless we become like children, we will never enter the kingdom of God. May I always be as eager and open as my daughter to experience God's kingdom.

Ezekiel 18:1–10,13b,30–32
Psalm 51:12–13,14–15,18–19
Matthew 19:13–15

*"Whoever eats my flesh and drinks my blood remains in me and
I in him."*
—JOHN 6:54

I often long for Holy Communion—to feel the wafer on my
tongue and the wine on my lips. It is a reminder of to whom I
belong. It gives me life, the strength to go on, and comfort
for the journey.

Proverbs 9:1–6
Psalm 34:2–3,4–5, 6–7 (9a)
Ephesians 5:15–20
John 6:51–58

*"If you wish to be perfect, go, sell what you have and give to the poor,
and you will have treasure in heaven. Then come, follow me."*
—MATTHEW 19:21

What are we willing to give up to follow Christ? Our wealth?
Our dreams? Everything we own? What is holding us back?
Our lack of compassion? Our need for security? Our pride?
Our need for status? What do we need to give up, let go of,
sacrifice, for something far greater?

Ezekiel 24:15–23
Deuteronomy 32:18–19,20,21
Matthew 19:16–22

"It will be hard for one who is rich to enter the Kingdom of heaven."
—MATTHEW 19:23

After years of financial struggle, my husband and I recently received a small inheritance. We are grateful that it's enough for us to pay off some debt and possibly move into a larger house. But I wonder what it will do to my spiritual life. For years I have begged God to give us financial relief. Now that we feel more secure, will I stop seeking and searching for God?

Ezekiel 28:1–10
Deuteronomy 32:26–27ab,27cd–28,30,35cd–36ab
Matthew 19:23–30

"Are you envious because I am generous? Thus, the last will be first, and the first will be last."
—MATTHEW 20:15–16

Again and again, Jesus tears down systems we are obsessed with, such as hierarchy and meritocracy. Jesus tells parables of how the kingdom of God levels the playing field. In this parable, a landowner hires fieldworkers and offers them the usual daily wage. Then he hires other workers for an hour of work—but he pays them the same. The workers who worked longer hours complain, and the landowner responds by telling them they were paid what they had agreed—and that they should just take their wages and go. Aren't we like that sometimes? We see what God has given others and complain, thinking that we deserve it more. Maybe we should see it as a testament to God's generosity, and be grateful.

Ezekiel 34:1–11
Psalm 23:1–3a,3b–4,5,6
Matthew 20:1–16

I will give you a new heart and place a new spirit within you.
—EZEKIEL 36:26

Research varies, but some studies report that more than
three-quarters of heart bypass patients experience major
depression after surgery. No one knows why. But I wonder if
it's because we think of our hearts as our souls—surgery on
our hearts is surgery on who we are. Replacing an old heart
with a new one is no small task. Poet Federico Garcia Lorca,
in his poem "New Heart," writes, "Like a snake, my heart /
has shed its skin. / I hold it there in my hand, full of honey
and wounds."

Ezekiel 36:23–28
Psalm 51:12–13,14–15,18–19
Matthew 22:1–14

"Do you believe because I told you that I saw you under the fig tree? You will see greater things than this." . . . "Amen, amen, I say to you, you will see heaven opened and the angels of God ascending and descending on the Son of Man."
—JOHN 1:50–51

When we are sitting hopelessly in the therapist's office, when we get a scary diagnosis, when we are exhausted by trying to figure it all out, and when all seems lost, these are the moments when Christ is asking us, "Do you believe?"

Revelation 21:9b–14
Psalm 145:10–11,12–13,17–18
John 1:45–51

⇒ 265 ⇐

Saturday

AUGUST 25

• ST. LOUIS • ST. JOSEPH CALASANZ, PRIEST •

"The greatest among you must be your servant. Whoever exalts himself will be humbled; but whoever humbles himself will be exalted."
—MATTHEW 23:11–12

It is a rare leader who has the integrity, humility, wisdom, and servant's heart to earn my respect. The real leaders—the ones who inspire me—are the ones who don't really want to be leaders at all. They are the leaders who are unassuming, who want to serve people. Not those who are trying to be the greatest for the glory of it all, who are just in it for themselves, and whose ambition and arrogance will cause their downfall in the end.

Ezekiel 43:1–7ab
Psalm 85:9ab and 10,11–12,13–14
Matthew 23:1–12

Jesus then said to the Twelve, "Do you also want to leave?" Simon Peter
answered him, "Master, to whom shall we go?"
—JOHN 6:67–68

Many disciples had already left and returned to their former
way of life. But when Jesus asked the twelve if they wanted to
leave too, they chose to stay. They believed Jesus had the
words of eternal life. Where else would they find this? They
had nowhere else to go. So they followed him to the end,
which was really the beginning.

Joshua 24:1–2a,15–17,18b
Psalm 34:2–3,16–17,18–19,20–21 (9a)
Ephesians 5:21–32 or 5:2a,25–32
John 6:60–69

Monday

AUGUST 27

• ST. MONICA •

Sing to the LORD a new song;
sing to the LORD, all you lands.
Sing to the LORD; bless his name.
—PSALM 96:1

The psalms are filled with references to singing and songs.
One of my favorite U2 songs is based on Psalm 40, which
ends with the refrain, "How long to sing this song?" Last
night my husband and I sat on a beach in Michigan and
watched the sun set. So many years we have cried to God,
"How long? How long to sing this song?" as we struggled
with our marriage. But last night, as we watched the sun set
with our arms around each other, we finally felt free from
resentment, anger, and hurt. During those times when you
find yourself saying, "How long . . .?" remember there will
come a time when you will be singing a new song.

2 Thessalonians 1:1–5,11–12
Psalm 96:1–2a,2b–3,4–5
Matthew 23:13–22

Tuesday

AUGUST 28

• ST. AUGUSTINE, BISHOP AND DOCTOR OF THE CHURCH •

*"Blind Pharisee, cleanse the inside of the cup, so that the outside also
may be clean."*
—MATTHEW 23:26

The inside of my car is a disaster. I'm trying to teach our
daughter to put her broken crayons, empty juice boxes, and
half-eaten French fries in the plastic bag I keep on the back
floor, but it's a never-ending battle. The outside of my car
doesn't look half bad, though! Sometimes my life is sort of
like my car. I may look presentable on the outside. I have
learned to keep up appearances. But the inside of my life is a
disaster. Christ is asking us to start with the inside. To
vacuum out the garbage dump first—to attend to the
important things. Then the outside will take care of itself.

2 Thessalonians 2:1–3a,14–17
Psalm 96:10,11–12,13
Matthew 23:23–26

Wednesday

AUGUST 29

• THE PASSION OF ST. JOHN THE BAPTIST •

John had said to Herod, "It is not lawful to have your brother's wife."
—MARK 6:18

John confronted Herod and made him face his sin. It must have been hard for him, knowing that Herod had so much power. And yet John wasn't going to let Herod get away with his adultery. In the end, it cost John his life. How far are we willing to go to speak the truth?

2 Thessalonians 3:6–10,16–18
Psalm 128:1–2,4–5
Mark 6:17–29

AUGUST 30

Jesus said to his disciples, "Stay awake!"
—MATTHEW 24:42

How often do we go through the day on autopilot? Grocery shopping, commuting to work, attending meetings, answering e-mails, surfing the Internet, paying bills, cooking dinner, getting children ready for bed. In such a busy existence, it takes effort to stay awake, to find real meaning, to see God's work in the world. But this is one of the most important things: to stay awake. Don't let life pass by in a whirlwind. Go on a silent retreat. Write in a journal. Pray. Meditate. Take a walk. Go to Mass. We need to shake ourselves out of our slumber and experience God in this beautiful, beautiful world. Stay awake!

1 Corinthians 1:1–9
Psalm 145:2–3,4–5,6–7
Matthew 24:42–51

AUGUST 31

The Lord brings to naught the plans of nations;
he foils the designs of peoples.
But the plan of the Lord stands forever;
the design of his heart, through all generations.
—PSALM 33:10–11

In her book *Bird by Bird*, Anne Lamott writes, "If you want to make God laugh, tell her your plans." How many of us are living the lives that we had planned? How many times have we lamented, "This is not what I expected"? God's plans are not our plans. We can see only our story, but we are part of a grander narrative, and God is working out his plan through us.

1 Corinthians 1:17–25
Psalm 33:1–2,4–5,10–11
Matthew 25:1–13

SEPTEMBER 1

*God chose the foolish of the world to shame the wise, and God chose the
weak of the world to shame the strong.*
—1 CORINTHIANS 1:27

Here's good news for most of us: God chooses the foolish,
the weak, the nobodies. What puts us behind in our society
puts us ahead in God's economy. Maybe God chooses the
weak so that there's no doubt who will get the glory.

1 Corinthians 1:26–31
Psalm 33:12–13,18–19,20–21
Matthew 25:14–30

⇒ 273 ⇐

All good giving and every perfect gift is from above, coming down from the Father of lights.
—JAMES 1:17

I often fall into the trap of thinking that my possessions are my own—that I have earned what I have by working hard. When will I learn that everything I have is from God? And when will I develop the daily habit of thanking God for these gifts?

Deuteronomy 4:1–2,6–8
Psalm 15:2–3,3–4,4–5 (1a)
James 1:17–18,21b–22,27
Mark 7:1–8,14–15,21–23

Monday

SEPTEMBER 3

• ST. GREGORY THE GREAT, POPE AND DOCTOR OF THE CHURCH •
• LABOR DAY •

I came to you in weakness and fear and much trembling, and my message
and my proclamation were not with persuasive words of wisdom, but
with a demonstration of spirit and power, so that your faith might rest
not on human wisdom but on the power of God.
—1 CORINTHIANS 2:3–5

Do you feel inadequate, afraid, shaky, nervous, having no
idea what you're doing or how you're going to do it? Then,
congratulations! God can work through you. It's not your
wisdom or talent that is going to spread the Good News, but
God's power working through you.

1 Corinthians 2:1–5
Psalm 119:97,98,99,100,101,102
Luke 4:16–30

We have not received the spirit of the world but the Spirit who is from God, so that we may understand the things freely given us by God.
—1 CORINTHIANS 2:12

The word *Spirit* in the New Testament comes from the Greek word *pneuma*, which means "breath, spirit, wind." Wind is the movement of air caused by the uneven heating of the earth by the sun. We use wind to fly kites and sail boats. We feel the summer breeze on our faces and in our hair. But its power can also provide electricity, blow down buildings, impact ocean currents, and change geography. When we are confirmed, the bishop anoints us with oil, saying, "Be sealed with the gift of the Holy Spirit." May we always remember that we are granted a powerful gift that can change the current of our lives and the landscape of our souls.

1 Corinthians 2:10b–16
Psalm 145:8–9,10–11,12–13ab,13cd–14
Luke 4:31–37

SEPTEMBER 5

At daybreak, Jesus left and went to a deserted place.
—LUKE 4:42

After casting out demons and curing the sick, Jesus needed a break. So, he left and went to a deserted place. But the crowds followed him and didn't allow him to leave. Every mother of young children knows how he felt. Sometimes you just need space, but even going to the bathroom alone is impossible because your kid stands outside the door and yells, "Mommy, what are you doing in there?!" We need to fight for our alone time because it's good for our souls. These are the times when we reconnect with God, listen for his voice, and gather the strength to accomplish the work he has for us to do.

1 Corinthians 3:1–9
Psalm 33:12–13,14–15,20–21
Luke 4:38–44

SEPTEMBER 6

*If anyone among you considers himself wise in this age, let him become a
fool, so as to become wise.*
—1 CORINTHIANS 3:18

You know the type: the people who think they know
everything. I had a boss once who was really good at talking.
He could make anything sound good. He got promoted
because he was "good in front of clients." He always sounded
good, but he often spouted off bad ideas, got the facts
wrong, and made empty promises to clients. Plus, he was
arrogant. I kept thinking that if that's the type of person I had
to be to get promoted, then count me out. There are many
people who think they are wise. But those who go against
the "wisdom" of the world are the ones who are truly wise.

1 Corinthians 3:18–23
Psalm 24:1bc–2,3–4ab,5–6
Luke 5:1–11

He will bring to light what is hidden in darkness.
—1 CORINTHIANS 4:5

When we know God loves us unconditionally, we finally have the freedom to shine the light on our darkness. That's what confession is all about, isn't it? We confess our sins, or tell someone about our darkest secret or something we feel ashamed about. By confessing it we bring it into the light, where it can be healed by the brilliant warmth of the sun.

1 Corinthians 4:1–5
Psalm 37:3–4,5–6,27–28,39–40
Luke 5:33–39

We know that all things work for good for those who love God, who are
called according to his purpose.
—ROMANS 8:28

Mary probably wondered how her life had turned into such a
mess. A virgin. Pregnant. Joseph was going to quietly break
up with her. How many times have we felt that there was no
way out? No way through the mess, no way to make things
all right again. Yet in the end God was using Mary to bring a
Savior into the world. All things work together for good.
The novelist Mary Doria Russell, in a radio interview, said,
"God paints on a vast canvas, and his paintbrush is time." All
these bad things in your life right now? God is using them to
create a work of art.

Micah 5:1–4a or Romans 8:28–30
Psalm 13:6ab,6c
Matthew 1:1–16,18–23 or 1:18–23

*Did not God choose those who are poor in the world to be rich in faith
and heirs of the kingdom that he promised to those who love him?*
—JAMES 2:5

Before I became Catholic, I attended a nondenominational
evangelical church. The church was filled with young,
beautiful urban professionals. One day, a homeless man
walked into the sanctuary. Dirt caked his pants and shoes, his
hair was disheveled, and he smelled. But he walked right to
the front and sat down in the front row, calmly, for the whole
service. Then he walked out. It was a shock to see a homeless
man in that setting, and I could tell that many people were
uncomfortable and anxious about his presence. Jesus says
that if we treat a poor person in shabby clothes worse than
someone with gold rings and fine clothes, we become judges
with evil designs.

Isaiah 35:4–7a
Psalm 146:6–7,8–9,9–10 (1b)
James 2:1–5
Mark 7:31–37

SEPTEMBER 10

Your boasting is not appropriate. Do you not know that a little yeast leavens all the dough?
—1 CORINTHIANS 5:6

In today's publishing market, authors must be willing to promote themselves and their books. I find it difficult to find the balance between promotion and what feels like boasting.

Some people seem to have no problem promoting themselves or their books endlessly on Facebook, Twitter, and Instagram, but to be honest, I think it often backfires. People don't want to constantly hear from you about how great you are. Ultimately, the work must speak for itself.

1 Corinthians 5:1–8
Psalm 5:5–6,7,12
Luke 6:6–11

SEPTEMBER 11

And he came down with them and stood on a stretch of level ground.
—LUKE 6:17

Jesus went to a mountain to pray, and the next day he chose his twelve disciples. Then he came down the mountain with them and stood on a stretch of level ground. I love that Jesus stood on equal footing with his disciples. Jesus became one of us—was born like us, was a child like us, grew into an adult like us. Because he stands with us on a stretch of level ground, he understands our pain, suffering, joy, fears.

He is with us.

1 Corinthians 6:1–11
Psalm 149:1b–2,3–4,5–6a and 9b
Luke 6:12–19

SEPTEMBER 12

• THE MOST HOLY NAME OF MARY •

"Woe to you who are rich,
for you have received your consolation."
—LUKE 6:24

A synonym for the word *consolation* is "comfort." Jesus is warning the rich that their comfortable lives may lull them into thinking they do not need a Savior. How often do we envy those—even friends—who have more money than we do? They take relaxing vacations by the beach, they have bigger houses, and they probably don't worry about having enough money for retirement. And yet, if we had more money, would we miss out on the consolation that comes only from God?

1 Corinthians 7:25–31
Psalm 45:11–12,14–15,16–17
Luke 6:20–26

Knowledge inflates with pride, but love builds up.
—1 CORINTHIANS 8:1B

I was at a writers' conference a few years ago, overwhelmed and in awe of the talent and knowledge of the other writers who were speaking or leading workshops. At the same time, I became deeply discouraged that I hadn't yet achieved the success I wanted, and despair that I might never become a successful writer. Then I listened to a talk given by James McBride, author of the memoir *The Color of Water*. He talked about his writing and his success, and then he said, "You know, success is great, I am thankful for it, but the most important thing is getting up every day and asking yourself, 'Who can I love today?'" All of a sudden, my yearning for success and my frustrated ambition were put into perspective. Love trumps success. I try to remember that every day.

1 Corinthians 8:1b–7,11–13
Psalm 139:1b–3,13–14ab,23–24
Luke 6:27–38

⇉ 285 ⇇

For God so loved the world that he gave his only Son, so that everyone who believes in him might not perish but might have eternal life.
—JOHN 3:16

John 3:16 is probably the most famous verse in the Bible. You see it on placards in the crowds of televised sporting events. Most kids (Protestant kids, anyway) have it memorized by age five. It's on key chains, coffee mugs, and bumper stickers. It encapsulates the core message of Christianity. And yet, many people focus on the last part of the verse: "he gave his only Son, so that everyone who believes in him might not perish but might have eternal life." But the beginning says, "For God so loved the world . . ." *Loved.* All of this—Jesus, the cross, eternal life—comes from God's love. Think on that for a while.

Numbers 21:4b–9
Psalm 78:1bc–2,34–35,36–37,38
Philippians 2:6–11
John 3:13–17

SEPTEMBER 15

• OUR LADY OF SORROWS •

"Woman, behold, your son."
—JOHN 19:26

I can't imagine losing a child. I've heard it's the deepest grief you can experience. Mary stands at the foot of the cross, watching her son die. And Jesus, as he is dying, worries about who will take care of his mother. He says to one of his disciples, "Behold your mother" as he hands over the care of his mother to someone he loves. I find this part of the Crucifixion story touching. In his final hour, in his pain, he cares tenderly for his grieving mother. Jesus lived with human emotions and grief, just as we do.

1 Corinthians 10:14–22
Psalm 116:12–13,17–18
John 19:25–27 or Luke 2:33–35

SEPTEMBER 16

• TWENTY-FOURTH SUNDAY IN ORDINARY TIME •

*If a brother or sister has nothing to wear and has no food for the day,
and one of you says to them, "Go in peace, keep warm, and eat well," but
you do not give them the necessities of the body, what good is it?*
—JAMES 2:15–16

I have attended churches that kept their distance from the
poor—congregations that were uncomfortable if someone
who wasn't dressed right walked through the sanctuary
doors. Such believers avoid those in need. They might write
checks to charity, but they have no friends or acquaintances
outside their socioeconomic class. The writer of the book of
James says, What's the point? If you can't bother, then don't
call yourself a Christian.

Isaiah 50:5–9a
Psalm 116:1–2,3–4,5–6,8–9 (9)
James 2:14–18
Mark 8:27–35

SEPTEMBER 17

• ST. ROBERT BELLARMINE, BISHOP AND DOCTOR OF THE CHURCH •

In giving this instruction, I do not praise the fact that your meetings are doing more harm than good.
—1 CORINTHIANS 11:17

The Corinthian church had turned into a sort of fractured social club. The wealthy members were bringing food to the Lord's supper and eating it and getting drunk, while the poor went hungry and were embarrassed. Not exactly the unity God had in mind. Paul tells them to cut it out, that when they come together they should be focusing on remembering Christ and proclaiming the death of the Lord until he comes. What divides us from others in the church? How can we find unity with them?

1 Corinthians 11:17–26,33
Psalm 40:7–8a,8b–9,10,17
Luke 7:1–10

SEPTEMBER 18

As a body is one though it has many parts, and all the parts of the body,
though many, are one body, so also Christ.
—1 CORINTHIANS 12:12

Those who have had a limb amputated may experience
phantom pain: pain that feels as if it's coming from the limb
that was amputated. Doctors used to think this was a
psychological phenomenon, but now they understand that
this pain originates in the spinal cord and brain. The brain
gets confused when it is no longer receiving messages from
the nerves of the amputated limb, so it goes haywire. The
apostle Paul said that the Church is like a body. We are all
one. And if one person is hurting, or lost, or alone, it
reverberates throughout the whole body. That's why we need
to care for one another as if we are caring for
ourselves—because we are.

1 Corinthians 12:12–14,27–31a
Psalm 100:1b–2,3,4,5
Luke 7:11–17

Wednesday
SEPTEMBER 19

So faith, hope, love remain, these three; but the greatest of these is love.
—1 CORINTHIANS 13:13

When Desta was four or five she started telling me, at bedtime, how much she loved me. She would say, "Mommy, I will love you for 100 years." In response, I would then say to her, "Desta, I will love you for 1,000 years," and then she would say, "Mommy, I will love you for a million years." I'd respond, "And then I will love you for a gazillion years." "Mommy, I will love you for a gazillion, million years." One day, she came home from school and said, "Mommy, did you know that infinity is a number?" "Yes, I did know that." "Well," she said, "I will love you for infinity." She had already learned that, truly, the greatest thing is love.

1 Corinthians 12:31—13:13
Psalm 33:2–3,4–5,12 and 22
Luke 7:31–35

SEPTEMBER 20

• ST. ANDREW KIM TAE-GŎN, PRIEST AND MARTYR, ST. PAUL CHŎNG
HA-SANG, AND COMPANIONS, MARTYRS •

"But the one to whom little is forgiven, loves little."
—LUKE 7:47

Just as those who hike through the desert know the value of a cup of water, and those who have cancer in their bones know what a gift it is to get a drip of morphine, and those who live in solitary confinement know the importance of being touched by another human being, so, too, those who have fallen the furthest from God understand the power of God's forgiveness. They anoint his feet with oil and weep. They are humbled to their bones and forever changed. And they want others to experience the same deep, deep love of God.

1 Corinthians 15:1–11
Psalm 118:1b–2,16ab–17,28
Luke 7:36–50

While he was at table in his house, many tax collectors and sinners came
and sat with Jesus and his disciples.
—MATTHEW 9:11

We will be moving into a new house soon, and for the first
time in many years, I will have a dining room. I'm looking
forward to buying a table and chairs and hosting dinner
parties. It's interesting that the word *hospitality* comes from
the Latin *hospes*, which is also the root word of *hospital* and
hospice. In this passage, tax collectors and sinners came and
sat with Jesus at the table. They were imperfect, broken, and
sick, and yet they were drawn to Jesus because they knew he
would welcome them and heal them. I want my dining room
table to be a place that feels safe, where all of us—friends,
family, strangers—can break bread together despite our
imperfections, mistakes, sins, and wounds.

Ephesians 4:1–7,11–13
Psalm 19:2–3,4–5
Matthew 9:9–13

SEPTEMBER 22

What you sow is not brought to life unless it dies. And what you sow is not the body that is to be but a bare kernel of wheat, perhaps . . .
—1 CORINTHIANS 15:36–37

Paul wrote to the Corinthians about what happens when we die. Some were wondering what kind of body they would have. But Paul called them fools. It's not about the body. Our bodies are like a bare kernel of wheat, which dies in order that something will grow from it. He wrote, "It is sown in a natural body; it is raised in a spiritual body." I think of this as I age and my body is dying bit by bit. We are constantly dying physically, but we are more than our bodies. John Updike wrote in his memoir, *Self-Consciousness*, "Each day, we wake slightly altered, and the person we were yesterday is dead, so why . . . be afraid of death, when death comes all the time?"

1 Corinthians 15:35–37,42–49
Psalm 56:10c–12,13–14
Luke 8:4–15

You do not possess because you do not ask. You ask but do not receive,
because you ask wrongly, to spend it on your passions.
—JAMES 4:2–3

God wants us to come to him with our requests, desires, and
needs. Bring all your cares to him. But be careful that you are
not asking out of selfishness or greed. God knows better than
to give his children something that will not be good
for them.

Wisdom 2:12,17–20
Psalm 54:3–4,5,6–8 (6b)
James 3:16—4:3
Mark 9:30–37

Monday

SEPTEMBER 24

Say not to your neighbor, "Go, and come again,
tomorrow I will give," when you can give at once.
Plot no evil against your neighbor,
against one who lives at peace with you.
—PROVERBS 3:28

The second of the great commandments is "Love your neighbor as yourself." So it's no surprise that Scripture often talks about how we treat our neighbors. "Neighbor" could be the person living next door or the colleague sitting next to you at work, or even the person standing next to you on the commuter train. Look around you. To whom can you be generous and kind today?

Proverbs 3:27–34
Psalm 15:2–3a,3bc–4ab,5
Luke 8:16–18

SEPTEMBER 25

*[Whoever] shuts his ear to the cry of the poor
will himself also call and not be heard.*
—PROVERBS 21:13

This year, my home, Chicago, is on track to have the
deadliest year in nearly two decades. Gun violence is out of
control in impoverished neighborhoods. The reasons for the
violence are complex, but I think it can be boiled down to
"the cry of the poor." Systematic injustice, lack of
opportunities, and unsafe and low-performing schools create
hopelessness, depression, anger, and fear. How can I respond
to the cry of the poor?

Proverbs 21:1–6,10–13
Psalm 119:1,27,30,34,35,44
Luke 8:19–21

SEPTEMBER 26

• SS. COSMAS AND DAMIAN, MARTYRS •

Give me neither poverty nor riches;
provide me only with the food I need.
—PROVERBS 30:8

Who doesn't fear not having enough money or success? But St. Ignatius of Loyola calls these "disordered attachments" that get in the way of our following God. To remind me of this, I keep St. Ignatius's meditation from the Spiritual Exercises next to my desk. In part, it says, "We should not fix our desires on health or sickness, wealth or poverty, success or failure, a long life or a short one. For everything has the potential of calling forth in us a deeper response to our life in God. Our only desire and our one choice should be this: I want and I choose what better leads to God's deepening his life in me."

Proverbs 30:5–9
Psalm 119:29,72,89,101,104,163
Luke 9:1–6

SEPTEMBER 27

• ST. VINCENT DE PAUL, PRIEST •

Vanity of vanities, says Qoheleth,
vanity of vanities! All things are vanity!
What profit has man from all the labor
which he toils at under the sun?
—ECCLESIASTES 1:2–3

Do you ever feel as if, no matter how hard you work, you never get ahead? That no matter how hard you try, it doesn't really matter? Solomon laments for all of us: "The sun rises and the sun goes down; then it presses on to the place where it rises." He's saying, "Every day is the same old, same old routine." We are spinning our wheels. If we focus only on our earthly toil, it will seem pointless. Our focus must embrace God's love and purpose for us.

Ecclesiastes 1:2–11
Psalm 90:3–4,5–6,12–13,14 and 17bc
Luke 9:7–9

• ST. WENCESLAUS, MARTYR • ST. LAWRENCE RUIZ AND COMPANIONS,
MARTYRS •

*He has made everything appropriate to its time, and has put the timeless
into their hearts, without man's ever discovering, from beginning to end,
the work which God has done.*
—ECCLESIASTES 3:11

There is a time for everything, Solomon says. A time to be
born, a time to die; a time to plant, and a time to uproot the
plant. . . . We are governed by time. Right now, I'm rushing
to get this writing done so I can go pick up my daughter
from school. A time to write, a time to do school pickup.
Our eyes are always on the clock. We rush from one thing to
the next. But God is beyond time. He has put the timeless
into our hearts. While we are rushing around doing our daily
tasks, God works quietly, slowly doing his work in us. We are
so busy we don't even notice.

Ecclesiastes 3:1–11
Psalm 144:1b and 2abc,3–4
Luke 9:18–22

SEPTEMBER 29

• SS. MICHAEL, GABRIEL, AND RAPHAEL, ARCHANGELS •

"Here is a true child of Israel. There is no duplicity in him."
—JOHN 1:47

"Purity of heart is to will one thing," wrote Søren Kierkegaard, the nineteenth-century Danish theologian and philosopher. He suggested that we are unable to be at peace with ourselves if there is inner strife—if our minds are pulling us in two directions at once. As it says in Matthew 6:24, "No one can serve two masters." God wants us to follow him with our whole hearts. Otherwise we will be dissatisfied, conflicted, confused. But if our minds and hearts are focused on one organizing purpose, we will be at peace.

Daniel 7:9–10,13–14 or
Revelation 12:7–12ab
Psalm 138:1–2ab,2cde–3,4–5
John 1:47–51

SEPTEMBER 30

*Come now, you rich, weep and wail over your impending miseries. Your
wealth has rotted away, your clothes have become moth-eaten, your gold
and silver have corroded.*
—JAMES 5:1–3

Jesus reminds us repeatedly that the wealthy aren't as
fortunate as they seem. Richard Rohr, in his book *Everything
Belongs*, writes, "We are at a symbolic disadvantage as a
wealthy culture. Jesus said that the rich man or woman will
find it hard to understand what he is talking about. The rich
can satisfy their loneliness and longing in false ways, in quick
fixes that avoid the necessary learning. . . . That's why the
poor have a head start. They can't resort to an instant fix. . . .
they remain empty whether they want to or not."

Numbers 11:25–29
Psalm 19:8,10,12–13,14 (9a)
James 5:1–6
Mark 9:38–43,45,47–48

Monday

OCTOBER 1

*Then Job began to tear his cloak and cut off his hair. He cast himself
prostrate upon the ground, and said, / "Naked I came forth from my
mother's womb, / and naked shall I go back again. / The LORD gave
and the LORD has taken away; / blessed be the name of the LORD!"*
—JOB 1:20,21

Satan said to God, "Sure, Job is faithful to you—because you
have given him everything, including a family and livestock
and wealth. Take that all away and see what happens!" God
called his bluff. He allowed Satan to take everything of Job's
except his life. We all know what happened. Job lost
everything, and yet—after much complaint and sorrow and
questioning—he praised God. He recognized all earthly gifts
as impermanent; he recognized himself as always naked
before the Divine. As we all are, even when we don't
recognize that truth.

Job 1:6–22
Psalm 17:1bcd,2–3,6–7
Luke 9:46–50

OCTOBER 2

Job opened his mouth and cursed his day. Job spoke out and said:
Perish the day on which I was born,
the night when they said, "The child is a boy!"
—JOB 3:1–3

In the Coen brothers' movie *A Serious Man*, the protagonist, Larry Gopnik, is a Job figure. Everything in his life is going wrong: his wife is having an affair; his deadbeat brother is living with him; he's having trouble at work. Like Job, Larry doesn't understand why. He hasn't done anything wrong to deserve his fate. He has been "a serious man." He goes from rabbi to rabbi, trying to find the answers, but the rabbis have none. Sometimes, when we feel most in need of answers, none are given. If you are in that place today, know that you are not alone.

Job 3:1–3,11–17,20–23
Psalm 88:2–3,4–5,6,7–8
Matthew 18:1–5,10

OCTOBER 3

*He does great things past finding out,
marvelous things beyond reckoning.*
—JOB 9:10

Job's friends question why he remains faithful to God after
his whole world has fallen apart. Job answers by trying to
describe God: God is wise in heart and mighty in strength.
He removes mountains before they know it. He alone
stretches out the heavens. Basically, his answer to them is
"Do you even understand how big God is?" One of my
favorite novels is C. S. Lewis's *Till We Have Faces*, a retelling
of the myth of Cupid and Psyche. The main character,
Orual, does not understand why she is ugly and her sister
Psyche is beautiful. She spends her whole life writing her
complaints to God. But when she is finally reading her
lifelong list of grievances, she falls silent. For as she is
face-to-face with God, his beauty and majesty are
her answer.

Job 9:1–12,14–16
Psalm 88:10bc–11,12–13,14–15
Luke 9:57–62

OCTOBER 4

• ST. FRANCIS OF ASSISI •

*"The harvest is abundant but the laborers are few; so ask the master of
the harvest to send out laborers for his harvest. Go on your way . . .
carry no money bag, no sack, no sandals."*
—LUKE 10:2–4

We are called to spread the Good News, but how often are
we weighed down by baggage? Maybe it's the idolatry of
success or the burden of too many possessions. Maybe it's
bitterness, anger, anxiety, or insecurity. Maybe our baggage is
simple complacency. We become too comfortable in our own
worlds and don't see that the harvest is abundant. How,
today, can we put down that baggage and enter God's fields?

Job 19:21–27
Psalm 27:7–8a,8b–9abc,13–14
Luke 10:1–12

O LORD, you have probed me and you know me;
you know when I sit and when I stand;
you understand my thoughts from afar.
My journeys and my rest you scrutinize,
with all my ways you are familiar.
—PSALM 139:1–3

There's no better feeling in the world than to feel truly known. It's also a bit disconcerting. After eleven years of marriage, my husband and I know each other well. Sometimes we can read each other's minds. He knows, through my silence or body language, if I'm stressed or upset. I can tell by the look on his face if he's feeling discouraged about work. God created us, and he knows us. He *really* knows us. How beautiful and horrifying is that?

Job 38:1,12–21; 40:3–5
Psalm 139:1–3,7–8,9–10,13–14ab
Luke 10:13–16

Saturday

OCTOBER 6

• ST. BRUNO, PRIEST • BLESSED MARIE-ROSE DUROCHER, VIRGIN •

I know that you can do all things,
and that no purpose of yours can be hindered.
I have dealt with great things that I do not understand;
things too wonderful for me, which I cannot know.
—JOB 42:2–3

God uses everything: our mistakes and ignorance; our
suffering and joy; our distractions, laziness, willfulness. If you
think you've missed God's will for you, don't worry. No
purpose of God can be hindered. He will use it all for your
good and his glory.

Job 42:1–3,5–6,12–17
Psalm 119:66,71,75,91,125,130
Luke 10:17–24

"For this reason a man shall leave his father and mother and
be joined to his wife, and the two shall become one flesh."
—MARK 10:7–8

It took me a long time to get married, in part because I was
afraid, wary of losing my freedom and independence. My
husband felt that way too. But when we finally met each
other, we were engaged in three months and married in eight
months. I think both of us were ready to "leave father and
mother and be joined," but it hasn't been easy to meld two
hearts, minds, and bodies. Both of us have entered a new
existence and experienced a fundamental change in life
orientation, in which God has brought our paths and gifts
together.

Genesis 2:18–24
Psalm 128:1–2,3,4–5,6
Hebrews 2:9–11
Mark 10:2–16 or 10:2–12

OCTOBER 8

Am I now currying favor with human beings or God?
—GALATIANS 1:10

Sometimes, following Christ means looking foolish or reckless or disappointing in the eyes of those around us. Pleasing people can take subtle forms. We don't want to rock the boat or hurt someone's feelings. We don't want to disappoint someone. How many people have chosen careers based on what their parents wanted and not what they were called to do? They spend years feeling frustrated and bitter, trying to unravel the choices they have made. It takes courage to follow Christ despite others' disappointment or disapproval.

Galatians 1:6–12
Psalm 111:1b–2,7–8,9 and 10c
Luke 10:25–37

Martha, burdened with much serving, came to him and said, "Lord, do you not care that my sister has left me by myself to do the serving?"
—LUKE 10:40

How much time do we spend doing things that don't matter? Martha was running around preparing a meal while Mary was sitting at the feet of Jesus, listening. Perturbed, Martha complains to Jesus, but he tells her, "Mary has chosen the better part and it will not be taken from her." The better part. We rush through our lives taking care of the urgent things and miss the better part. What "better part" are you missing out on today?

Galatians 1:13–24
Psalm 139:1b–3,13–14ab,14c–15
Luke 10:38–42

OCTOBER 10

"Give us each day our daily bread."
—LUKE 11:3

One thing that has helped me when financial anxiety gets
the best of me is to remind myself, "Today, we have enough.
Enough food in the pantry. Enough to pay for gas. Enough to
get through until tomorrow." Like a recovering alcoholic who
focuses on staying sober one day at a time, I limit my focus
to just one day. God gives us our daily bread—not our
monthly bread, or yearly bread, or lifetime bread. He gives
us just what we need, for today. That is enough.

Galatians 2:1–2,7–14
Psalm 117:1bc,2
Luke 11:1–4

"And I tell you, ask and you will receive; seek and you will find; knock and the door will be opened to you."
—LUKE 11:9

Ask and you shall receive. What will we receive? Do we even know what we need? Prayer is a conversation with God, but often we come to him asking for things we want instead of listening for his voice. In *The Way of the Heart: The Spirituality of the Desert Fathers and Mothers*, Henri J. M. Nouwen writes, "Through prayer we can carry in our heart all human pain and sorrow, all conflicts and agonies, all torture and war, all hunger, loneliness, and misery, not because of some great psychological or emotional capacity, but because God's heart has become one with ours." What do we receive in prayer? Whatever we need.

Galatians 3:1–5
Luke 1:69–70,71–72,73–75
Luke 11:5–13

"And that no one is justified before God by the law is clear, for the one who is righteous by faith will live."
—GALATIANS 3:11

How difficult it must have been for Jewish followers of Jesus to understand that their sacred law was not sufficient to give them life. Jesus came to provide a new way—one of faith. To be honest, it can be easier to live by rules; they tend to be black and white and specific—you're not required to think or discern. But there's also a downside—you aren't truly free. Christ ransomed us from the curse of the law, says Scripture. Living by faith is scarier sometimes than simply following rules, but people who live close to God do so by faith.

Galatians 3:7–14
Psalm 111:1b–2,3–4,5–6
Luke 11:15–26

OCTOBER 13

There is neither Jew nor Greek, there is neither slave nor free person, there is not male and female; for you are all one in Christ Jesus.
—GALATIANS 3:28

My grandfather Clair always saw the good in everyone. I remember him taking a local mentally-disabled boy fishing and befriending everyone within a five-mile radius of our home. It didn't matter if they were rich, poor, male, female, white, or black; to him, everyone was worthy of his time and kindness. The kingdom of God is like that. It's the great equalizer. In Christ's kingdom, there is no more racism, misogyny, slavery, and religious divisions. We are all one in Christ Jesus. I strive to be like my grandpa Clair, seeing the good in everyone.

Galatians 3:22–29
Psalm 105:2–3,4–5,6–7
Luke 11:27–28

Sunday

OCTOBER 14

• TWENTY-EIGHTH SUNDAY IN ORDINARY TIME •

"Amen, I say to you, there is no one who has given up house or brothers or sisters or mother or father or children or lands for my sake and for the sake of the gospel who will not receive a hundred times more now in this present age."
—MARK 10:29–30

A rich man came to Jesus and asked what he needed to do to be saved. "Go, sell what you have, and give to the poor, and you will have treasure in heaven; then come, follow me." But the rich man was not willing to sell his many possessions, so he walked away. What is God asking you to give up to follow him? Can you let it go? Can you trust that what you gain by following Christ will be much greater?

Wisdom 7:7–11
Psalm 90:12–13,14–15,16–17 (14)
Hebrews 4:12–13
Mark 10:17–30 or 10:17–27

He raises up the lowly from the dust;
from the dunghill he lifts up the poor.
—PSALM 113:7

There's a four-mile-square garbage dump in Nicaragua called
La Chureca. One thousand people, called Churequeros, live
and work on the "City of Trash" every day. They dig through
rotting garbage to find food, as well as pieces of plastic and
glass to sell for recycling. They build homes with the trash
they find. The future for the children there is bleak. After the
children complete school, most of them end up working long
hours in the landfill to help support their families. But many
ministries are trying to help the Churequeros. They have
built schools and clinics and have helped prevent the sexual
abuse many of the kids have experienced. These ministry
workers are the hands and feet of Jesus, lifting up the poor
from the dunghill.

Galatians 4:22–24,26–27,31—5:1
Psalm 113:1b–2,3–4,5a and 6–7
Luke 11:29–32

—————————

⇒ 317 ⇐

Tuesday

OCTOBER 16

• ST. HEDWIG, RELIGIOUS * ST. MARGARET MARY ALACOQUE, VIRGIN •

For freedom Christ set us free; so stand firm and do not submit again to the yoke of slavery.
—GALATIANS 5:1

Randall Lee Church spent years in prison for fatally stabbing a man—he says in self-defense. He was released in April 2011, but after just ninety-six days of freedom, he intentionally set fire to an abandoned house. He admitted his crime to police. It turns out that he wanted to go back to prison and back to his job at his former prison unit. Many former inmates can't handle being on "the outside." Aren't we often like these prisoners? We find freedom in Christ and yet go back to our destructive, sinful ways—maybe because it's what we are used to. Freedom can be scary and hard. Embrace your freedom in Christ. You are a new creation.

Galatians 5:1–6
Psalm 119:41,43,44,45,47,48
Luke 11:37–41

OCTOBER 17

• ST. IGNATIUS OF ANTIOCH, BISHOP AND MARTYR •

Now the works of the flesh are obvious: immorality, impurity, licentiousness, idolatry, sorcery, hatreds, rivalry, jealousy, outbursts of fury, acts of selfishness, dissensions, factions, occasions of envy, drinking bouts, orgies, and the like.
—GALATIANS 5:19–21

Whew, that's a long list. I must say, I don't struggle with drinking bouts, orgies, or licentiousness, and I've never dabbled in sorcery. But the rest of the list? Yep—I have been guilty. Paul says that we who belong to Christ Jesus have crucified our flesh with its passions and desires. If we live in the Spirit, let us also follow the Spirit. Lord, help me live in the Spirit and not the flesh.

Galatians 5:18–25
Psalm 1:1–2,3,4 and 6
Luke 11:42–46

⇒ 319 ⇐

*Demas, enamored of the present world, deserted me and went
to Thessalonica.*
—2 TIMOTHY 4:10

Wouldn't you hate to be Demas, known for being "enamored
of the present world"? St. John Chrysostom paraphrased this
passage as, "Having loved ease and safety, chose rather to live
daintily at home than to suffer affliction, than to endure
hardship, with me, and with me to bear these present
dangers." Demas chose safety and comfort instead of
continuing in the work of the Lord. I think there's a bit of
Demas in all of us. I can quickly become enamored with the
present world and choose ease and safety—living daintily at
home. Do we want to be like Demas, or Paul?

2 Timothy 4:10–17b
Psalm 145:10–11,12–13,17–18
Luke 10:1–9

Friday

OCTOBER 19

• SS. ISAAC JOGUES AND JOHN DE BRÉBEUF, PRIESTS, AND COMPANIONS, MARTYRS •

"Are not five sparrows sold for two small coins? Yet not one of them has escaped the notice of God . . . Do not be afraid. You are worth more than many sparrows."
—LUKE 12:6–7

The tiny backyard at our new house is filled with fruit trees, vines, a birdbath, and plants I have yet to identify. It's home to many birds and squirrels and even a black cat (hunting the poor little birds, I presume). Today I saw a huge cardinal. During breakfast we watch the birds flit around playfully. We have named the squirrels—one is called "Fatty." Sometimes it's hard to comprehend that God cares for us. The world is vast—why would he care for little old me? But he does. And he cares for Fatty and the huge cardinal and the ordinary sparrows, too, flitting around without a care in the world.

Ephesians 1:11–14
Psalm 33:1–2,4–5,12–13
Luke 12:1–7

When I behold your heavens, the work of your fingers,
the moon and the stars which you set in place—
What is man that you should be mindful of him?
—PSALM 8:4–5

Most of us have experienced awe: when we first saw the mountains, or a meteor shower, or a newborn baby. "Awe is the feeling of being in the presence of something vast or beyond human scale, that transcends our current understanding of things," says psychologist Dacher Keltner, a pioneer in the study of emotions who started a research project to learn more about awe. It turns out that awe is good for us; it can alleviate symptoms of PTSD, make us nicer and happier, and bind us together. The psalmist, in awe of God's creation, wondered how such an amazing God could care about us. But he does. And that is awesome.

Ephesians 1:15–23
Psalm 8:2–3ab,4–5,6–7
Luke 12:8–12

Because of his affliction
he shall see the light in fullness of days;
through his suffering, my servant shall justify many,
and their guilt he shall bear.
—ISAIAH 53:11

When we're in pain, we pray, just as Jesus prayed in the garden, "God, please take this cup from me." Likewise, we say with Jesus, "Your will be done" and then wait and see how God can redeem our suffering.

Isaiah 53:10–11
Psalm 33:4–5,18–19,20,22 (22)
Hebrews 4:14–16
Mark 10:35–45 or 10:42–45

*But God, who is rich in mercy, because of the great love he had for us . . .
brought us to life with Christ (by grace you have been saved), raised us
up with him.*
—EPHESIANS 2:4–6

When Karol Wojtyla was at the university in Krakow, Nazis
entered Poland and immediately shut down the university. To
make a living and avoid deportation, he worked at a rock
quarry. During this dark time in his life, he met Jan
Tyranowski, a Catholic layman who played a part in his call
to the priesthood. He was "like a marvelous light at the
bottom of life, at a depth where night usually reigns," said
Karol, who went on to become Pope John Paul II. During
dark times, be encouraged by his story and message: "Do not
abandon yourselves to despair," he said. "We are the Easter
people, and hallelujah is our song."

Ephesians 2:1–10
Psalm 100:1b–2,3,4ab,4c–5
Luke 12:13–21

Tuesday

OCTOBER 23

• ST. JOHN OF CAPISTRANO, PRIEST •

"Blessed are those servants whom the master finds vigilant on his arrival."
—LUKE 12:37

I hate being late. I'm usually the first one to get to a restaurant to get a table before the rest of the party arrives. And when I'm waiting, I'm constantly on the lookout—for my friends to walk in the door or for a glimpse of their car pulling up outside. I'm aware of everything around me when I anticipate the arrival of a friend. This is how Jesus wants us to be: aware, alert, anticipating his presence. We don't want to miss it.

Ephesians 2:12–22
Psalm 85:9ab–10,11–12,13–14
Luke 12:35–38

"Much will be required of the person entrusted with much, and still more will be demanded of the person entrusted with more."
—LUKE 12:48

What has God given to you abundantly? Money? Musical talent? Knowledge? Time? Cooking skills? Compassion? Intelligence? Energy? God wants us to use the abundant gifts he has given us for his kingdom. How can you do that today?

Ephesians 3:2–12
Isaiah 12:2–3,4bcd,5–6
Luke 12:39–48

*Now to him who is able to accomplish far more than all we ask
or imagine . . .*
—EPHESIANS 3:20

Giordano Bruno was a sixteenth-century monk born ahead of
his time. Until the late 1500s, it was believed that the earth
was the center of the universe. In 1543, however, Nicolaus
Copernicus proposed that the sun was at the center of the
universe and everything else revolved around it. Bruno
adopted and expanded on this idea, believing there was no
end to the universe, just as there was no end to God. The
Catholic Church did not like his views. He was censured,
stripped of his position, and imprisoned. When Bruno was
questioned about his theory and its conflicts with Church
doctrine, he replied, "Your God is too small." Still, we often
struggle with a perception of God that limits us.

Ephesians 3:14–21
Psalm 33:1–2,4–5,11–12,18–19
Luke 12:49–53

OCTOBER 26

Live in a manner worthy of the call you have received, with all humility and gentleness, with patience, bearing with one another through love, striving to preserve the unity of the spirit.
—EPHESIANS 4:1–3

If you ever watch programs on HGTV, you've heard the term "load-bearing wall." That's the wall in a house that is holding up the rest of the structure. The word *bear* means "to support." It also means "to endure." When we endure one another—with all our imperfections, quirks, disagreements—we are helping hold up the body of Christ. I admit, I flee when things get difficult in a relationship. But the older I get, the more I see the value of sticking around through thick and thin. Of having difficult conversations. Of reaching out to those I disagree with. Bearing with one another through love.

Ephesians 4:1–6
Psalm 24:1–2,3–4ab,5–6
Luke 12:54–59

OCTOBER 27

*The one who descended is also the one who ascended far above all the
heavens, that he might fill all things.*
—EPHESIANS 4:10

J. K. Rowling, author of the Harry Potter books, talks about
how she had to fail spectacularly in order to succeed. She
was a divorced, single mother who made only enough money
to keep her family from falling into homelessness. But it was
at that point in her life, when she had nothing left to lose,
that she had the courage to start writing *Harry Potter and the
Sorcerer's Stone*. She says that hitting rock bottom gave her the
foundation on which she could rise. Sometimes we have to
descend in order to ascend. If you're at rock bottom right
now, maybe that's the place where God can give you the
courage to become who you are meant to be.

Ephesians 4:7–16
Psalm 122:1–2,3–4ab,4cd–5
Luke 13:1–9

Sunday

OCTOBER 28

• THIRTIETH SUNDAY IN ORDINARY TIME •

So they called the blind man, saying to him, "Take courage; get up, Jesus is calling you."
—MARK 10:49

One of the priests at my church once said that love cures blindness. The playwright Tennessee Williams wrote that we never see anybody truly but all through our own egos—through vanity, fear, desire, competition. But that sometimes "there is a rare case of two people who love intensely enough to burn through all those layers of opacity and see each other's naked hearts." How many people passed by the blind man begging on the street, never noticing him? When the blind man heard Jesus coming, he called out, "Son of David, have pity on me!" Jesus stopped and saw him. "Master, I want to see," the blind man said. He received his sight and followed Jesus on his way.

Jeremiah 31:7–9
Psalm 126:1–2,2–3,4–5,6 (3)
Hebrews 5:1–6
Mark 10:46–52

For you were once darkness, but now you are light in the Lord. Live as children of light.
—EPHESIANS 5:8

I look out my kitchen window and see the sun coming up above our garage, painting the sky pale pink and orange. I'm anticipating the dark winter and wonder how we will get through it. What does it mean to live as children of light? Maybe it means that we live in hope and anticipation. That the sun always comes up. That the days will get longer. The light always comes. Always.

Ephesians 4:32—5:8
Psalm 1:1–2,3,4 and 6
Luke 13:10–17

OCTOBER 30

"What is the Kingdom of God like? To what can I compare it? It is like a mustard seed that a man took and planted in the garden. When it was fully grown, it became a large bush and 'the birds of the sky dwelt in its branches.'"

—LUKE 13:18–19

As I write this, the presidential election is a few days away. This election has been filled with hate, accusations, fear, anger, and smallness. It's easy to fall into despair that this is what our country has come to. But as Christians we can also be thankful, and hopeful, that this is not what the kingdom of God is like. The kingdom of God is life-giving, expansive, welcoming, inclusive. We must move toward those signs of the kingdom.

Ephesians 5:21–33 or 5:2a, 25–32
Psalm 128:1–2,3,4–5
Luke 13:18–21

"And people will come from the east and the west and from the north and the south and will recline at table in the Kingdom of God. For behold, some are last who will be first, and some are first who will be last."
—LUKE 13:29,30

It was 1999, and the war in the Balkans was raging. I stood in the airport waiting for a refugee family from Kosovo to come off the plane. I had signed up to sponsor them as they settled in America. Soon, I saw them: a couple in their late thirties with four little girls. They had one duffle bag between them. Over the years, I became close friends with this family, and they were generous, kind, and hardworking. The table in the kingdom of God is for everyone—the refugee, the dignitary, the politician. And I think the refugees will be sitting at the head of the table.

Ephesians 6:1–9
Psalm 145:10–11,12–13ab,13cd–14
Luke 13:22–30

Thursday

NOVEMBER 1

• ALL SAINTS •

"Blessed are the poor in spirit,
for theirs is the Kingdom of heaven."
—MATTHEW 5:3

"Poor in spirit" means that we know our need for God. We
realize our hunger, our yearning, our dependence. Sometimes
it takes an extraordinary experience to be jolted into
realizing our need for God. How are you poor in spirit
today? Know that you are blessed.

Revelation 7:2–4,9–14
Psalm 24:1b–2,3–4ab,5–6
1 John 3:1–3
Matthew 5:1–12a

NOVEMBER 2

• THE COMMEMORATION OF ALL THE FAITHFUL DEPARTED
(ALL SOULS' DAY) •

"For this is the will of my Father, that everyone who sees the Son and
believes in him may have eternal life, and I shall raise him on
the last day."
—JOHN 6:40

I learned of my mother's death as I was driving home to Iowa
for Christmas, on December 23, 2000. I called home in the
early evening, about an hour from my parents' house, to tell
them I would soon be home. Instead, my brother answered
the phone and told me my mother had died at 11:00 that
morning. Today, as we honor those who have died, I think of
my mother. We were both traveling home that day—me to
my childhood home, and my mother to her eternal home. I
thought my world had shattered that day, but I have hope
that on the last day we shall all be healed.

Wisdom 3:1–9
Psalm 23:1–3a,3b–4,5,6
Romans 5:5–11 or Romans 6:3–9
John 6:37–40
Other readings may be selected.

For to me life is Christ, and death is gain.
—PHILIPPIANS 1:21

I'm a hypochondriac. I feel a strange pain somewhere in my body, and I'm convinced I have cancer. I get a headache, and I think I'm having a stroke. I Google my symptoms and read medical articles on how long I have left to live. If Paul, the author of the letter to the Philippians, were living today, I'm fairly confident he wouldn't be Googling his symptoms. He was so enamored with Christ that it didn't really matter if he lived or died. If he lived, he would have more time to do Christ's work on this earth. But if he died, he would be with Christ. Maybe I should stop Googling symptoms and figure out how to be more like Paul.

Philippians 1:18b–26
Psalm 42:2,3,5cdef
Luke 14:1,7–11

*Therefore, you shall love the LORD, your God, with all your heart, and
with all your soul, and with all your strength.*
—DEUTERONOMY 6:5

God doesn't want our half-hearted commitment. He wants us
to be all in—passionately, totally, in all areas of our lives.
Pope Benedict XVI said, "Faith in the Lord is not something
that affects only our minds, the realm of intellectual
knowledge; rather, it is a change involving our whole
existence: our feelings, heart, mind, will, body, emotions and
human relationships. With faith, everything changes in us
and for us, and it reveals clearly our future destiny, the truth
of our vocation in history, the meaning of our lives, the joy
of being pilgrims en route to our heavenly homeland."

Deuteronomy 6:2–6
Psalm 18:2–3,3–4,47,51 (2)
Hebrews 7:23–28
Mark 12:28b–34

NOVEMBER 5

If there is any encouragement in Christ, any solace in love, any participation in the Spirit, any compassion and mercy, complete my joy by being of the same mind, with the same love, united in heart, thinking one thing. . . . [H]umbly regard others as more important than yourselves, each looking out not for his own interests, but also everyone for those of others.
—PHILIPPIANS 2:1–4

As I write this, we are coming to the end of the most rancorous, divisive presidential campaign in history. Even among those who call themselves Christians, there is a deep divide over what is right, what is truth, and what it means to live out our Christian values. I suspect God is mourning. But today's Scripture reminds me that I need to work hard for unity. I need to listen to the other side. To try to understand. To love my neighbors—no matter how they vote.

Philippians 2:1–4
Psalm 131:1bcde,2,3
Luke 14:12–14

NOVEMBER 6

*"Go out quickly into the streets and alleys of the town and bring in here
the poor and the crippled, the blind and the lame. . . . Go out to the
highways and hedgerows and make people come in that my home
may be filled."*
—LUKE 14:21,23

Jesus is telling a parable about a man who invited many to a
great feast. One by one, those invited decided that they
couldn't come; they were too busy. So the host told his
servant to invite those who were poor and crippled, blind
and lame. His servant kept inviting people until the house
was filled. How many times are we like those on the original
invitation list—so busy with our lives that we don't realize
the feast God is offering? I pray to be like the poor and the
crippled, the blind and the lame, who recognize their hunger
enough to accept the feast Christ offers.

Philippians 2:5–11
Psalm 22:26b–27,28–30ab,30e,31–32
Luke 14:15–24

NOVEMBER 7

"Whoever does not carry his own cross and come after me cannot be my disciple."
—LUKE 14:27

My therapist looked at me and said, "I sense a deep sadness in you. What do you think you need to grieve?" "Well," I replied, "how much time do you have? The list is long." For years, I have carried around the grief of lost dreams, of unfulfilled expectations, of deep disappointment. I keep wanting the Christian life to be easy and comfortable. When will I learn? Taking up my own cross means accepting that this life is filled with loss and suffering and unanswered questions. I have a spiritual mentor who says, "May you leave many tombs behind you." By that, he means that life is filled with loss and small deaths every day. Embrace the loss and believe that God can do something beautiful to redeem it.

Philippians 2:12–18
Psalm 27:1,4,13–14
Luke 14:25–33

NOVEMBER 8

*The tax collectors and sinners were all drawing near to listen to Jesus,
but the Pharisees and scribes began to complain, saying, "This man
welcomes sinners and eats with them."*

—LUKE 15:1–2

Twenty years ago, Father Greg Boyle went into the
gang-ridden part of Los Angeles and found hopelessness. So
he started Home Boy Industries, which ministers to former
gang members by educating them and giving them jobs. In
his book *Tattoos on the Heart*, he writes, "Jesus walks into a
room and loves what he finds there. Delights in it, in fact.
Maybe, He makes a beeline to the outcasts and chooses, in
them, to go where love has not yet arrived. His ways aren't
our ways, but they sure could be."

Philippians 3:3–8a
Psalm 105:2–3,4–5,6–7
Luke 15:1–10

God is our refuge and our strength,
an ever-present help in distress.
Therefore, we fear not, though the earth be shaken
and mountains plunge into the depths of the sea.

—PSALM 46:2–3

In the news today: riots about the recent presidential election, news of a 7.8 magnitude earthquake in New Zealand, more shootings in Chicago. In today's homily at Mass, the elderly priest reminded us that we don't have to fear. That he's seen a lot in his eighty-seven years and wants to remind us "younger folk" that it will be okay. We have survived other hard times, such as the Vietnam War and the terrorist attacks of September 11. What we need to do now is focus on what is in front of us—do the work that we are called to do and love the people we are called to love. Do not be afraid.

Ezekiel 47:1–2,8–9,12
Psalm 46:2–3,5–6,8–9
1 Corinthians 3:9c–11,16–17
John 2:13–22

NOVEMBER 10

• ST. LEO THE GREAT, POPE AND DOCTOR OF THE CHURCH •

*I have learned, in whatever situation I find myself, to be self-sufficient. I
know indeed how to live in humble circumstances; I know also how to
live with abundance. . . . I have the strength for everything through him
who empowers me.*
—PHILIPPIANS 4:12–13

My finances have been so tight that I once was overjoyed
when my then-boyfriend left a bunch of loose change on my
coffee table. He had plenty of money and thought a bunch
of quarters and dimes rattling around in his pocket was a
bother. To me, those coins were a windfall—enough money
to buy coffee the next morning. Now, years later, I have a
steady, well-paying job, and my husband and I just bought a
new house. But the million-dollar question is whether I will
continue to trust in God, to lean on his strength, if I'm down
to my last penny.

Philippians 4:10–19
Psalm 112:1b–2,5–6,8a and 9
Luke 16:9–15

NOVEMBER 11

• THIRTY-SECOND SUNDAY IN ORDINARY TIME •

In those days, Elijah the prophet went to Zarephath. As he arrived at the entrance of the city, a widow was gathering sticks there; he called out to her.
—1 KINGS 17:10

There are seventy-six verses about widows in the Bible; obviously, this group holds a special place in God's heart. In Jesus' day, when a woman's husband died, she was left with no economic support or safety net. Jesus protested the exploitation of widows (NAB Mark 12:40), praised the widow who gave her two last cents to the church (Mark 12:41–42), and healed a widow's son out of compassion for his mother (NAB Luke 7:11–17). Jesus sets an example of how we should care for the widows in our lives—those without support or means.

1 Kings 17:10–16
Psalm 146:7,8–9,9–10 (1b)
Hebrews 9:24–28
Mark 12:38–44 or 12:41–44

Monday

NOVEMBER 12

• ST. JOSAPHAT, BISHOP AND MARTYR •

And the Apostles said to the Lord, "Increase our faith." The Lord replied,
"If you have faith the size of a mustard seed, you would say to this
mulberry tree, 'Be uprooted and planted in the sea,' and it
would obey you."
—LUKE 17:5–6

The "tiny house movement" started after the Great
Recession. Homeowners no longer craved
McMansions—those huge, bloated, oversized houses in the
suburbs. Instead, they wanted something small, simple,
affordable, a home that wouldn't be burdensome. Some of
the tiny houses are only two hundred square feet! We tend to
think that bigger is always better, that the largest thing has
the most power. But in this Scripture, Christ is saying that
sometimes small things hold great value. Just a little faith is
enough. For a tiny bit of faith can grow into something that's
powerful enough to move mountains—or at least a
mulberry tree.

Titus 1:1–9
Psalm 24:1b–2, 3–4ab, 5–6
Luke 17:1–6

⇒ 345 ⇐

Tuesday

NOVEMBER 13

• ST. FRANCES XAVIER CABRINI, VIRGIN •

Take delight in the LORD,
and he will grant you your heart's requests.
—PSALM 37:4

Here, Scripture seems to be saying, if I delight in the Lord,
he will give me everything I want. Is God really a cosmic
Santa Claus, granting favors if I'm not on the naughty list?
Then where does that leave grace? I suspect that God is
saying that if we delight in him, it will be enough.
Everything else will fall away. All our worldly desires will
seem pale in comparison.

Titus 2:1–8,11–14
Psalm 37:3–4,18 and 23,27 and 29
Luke 17:7–10

⇒346⇐

NOVEMBER 14

*Even though I walk in the dark valley
I fear no evil; for you are at my side
With your rod and your staff
that give me courage.*
—PSALM 23:4

In the Terrence Malick film *Knight of Cups*, a priest tells the main character, "Seems you're alone. You're not. Even now He's taking your hand and guiding you by a way you cannot see. If you are unhappy, you shouldn't take it as a mark of God's disfavor. Just the contrary. It might be the very sign He loves you. He shows His love not by helping you avoid suffering, but by sending you suffering, by keeping you there. To suffer binds you to something higher than yourself, higher than your own will. Takes you from the world to find what lies beyond it." Are you walking through a dark valley today? Be comforted that God is taking your hand.

Titus 3:1–7
Psalm 23:1b–3a,3bc–4,5,6
Luke 17:11–19

"The coming of the Kingdom of God cannot be observed, and no one will announce, 'Look, here it is,' or, 'There it is.' For behold, the Kingdom of God is among you."

—LUKE 17:20–21

In Bob Dylan's song "Gotta Serve Somebody," he points out that a person does not go through life without serving somebody. It could be the devil, or it could be God, but we must decide. In these days, we experience so much upheaval in politics and policies. But the kingdom of God is among us, always, bringing about healing, beauty, salvation. Will we choose to serve that mission and vision?

Philemon 7–20
Psalm 146:7,8–9a,9bc–10
Luke 17:20–25

NOVEMBER 16

• ST. MARGARET OF SCOTLAND • ST. GERTRUDE, VIRGIN •

"Whoever seeks to preserve his life will lose it, but whoever loses it will save it."
—LUKE 17:33

Missionary Jim Elliot wanted to spread the Good News of the gospel to Ecuador's Huarani people, an isolated jungle tribe that feared outsiders. Elliot and four other missionaries tried to contact the Huaranis by dropping gifts from their small plane. Soon they felt comfortable enough to land their plane near the Huarani settlement and continue their efforts. But it was not to be. The Huaranis killed all five men. Years earlier, in his journal, Elliot had written, "He is no fool who gives what he cannot keep to gain that which he cannot lose." He was willing to risk his life to follow God. What is God calling you to do, and what are you willing to risk to follow him?

2 John 4–9
Psalm 119:1,2,10,11,17,18
Luke 17:26–37

NOVEMBER 17

• ST. ELIZABETH OF HUNGARY, RELIGIOUS •

*"Will not God then secure the rights of his chosen ones who call out to
him day and night? Will he be slow to answer them?"*
—LUKE 18:7

I have outgrown my childhood ideas of prayer, which
entailed kneeling beside my bed at night, asking God for
things that I thought would make me happy. Now my prayer
involves listening more than asking. And paying attention
throughout my day, not just kneeling at my bed at night. I
once heard that everyone should have a few "3:00 a.m.
friends"—people whom you trust so much that you can call
at any time, day or night. God wants us to trust him like that.
To know that we can pray at any time, day or night, and he
will hear us.

3 John 5–8
Psalm 112:1–2,3–4,5–6
Luke 18:1–8

*But the wise shall shine brightly
like the splendor of the firmament,
and those who lead the many to justice
shall be like the stars forever.*
—DANIEL 12:3

In 1966, Martin Luther King Jr. and seven hundred of his followers marched on Chicago's Southwest Side to protest housing discrimination. According to a Chicago Tribune article (7/28/16), thousands of white people lined the streets jeering, taunting, and throwing rocks and bottles. One rock hit King in the head, and he dropped to the ground. He was one of thirty people injured that day. When asked why he put himself at risk, he said, "I have to do this—to expose myself—to bring this hate into the open." Although the march turned violent, it did effect change. The Chicago Real Estate Board agreed to end its opposition to open-housing laws. King said that step was the "first in a 1,000-mile journey."

Daniel 12:1–3
Psalm 16:5,8,9–10,11 (1)
Hebrews 10:11–14,18
Mark 13:24–32

Jesus told him, "Have sight; your faith has saved you." He immediately received his sight and followed him, giving glory to God.
—LUKE 18:42–43

Sometimes I look back on my life and see what great things God has done. I may not have been healed from physical blindness, but I have been healed from the blindness of pride, envy, and selfishness. One year, my main prayer was, "God, take away my envy." Another year it was, "God, heal me from my pride." (Be careful what you pray for, especially when you ask God to heal you from your pride!) And yet another year, "Teach me how to love." Sometimes I forget to thank God for these things. But I am grateful. He is transforming me day by day. How has God healed you from your blindness?

Revelation 1:1–4; 2:1–5
Psalm 1:1–2,3,4 and 6
Luke 18:35–43

But Zacchaeus stood there and said to the Lord, "Behold, half of my possessions, Lord, I shall give to the poor, and if I have extorted anything from anyone I shall repay it four times over."

—LUKE 19:8

The Pharisees were incredulous that Jesus was going to eat with Zacchaeus, who was a tax collector. Tax collectors were known in those days for being corrupt and stealing from the poor. Why would Jesus want to hang out with someone like that? But Zacchaeus was repentant and contrite. Jesus knew his heart was in the right place. That is what God wants from us—a repentant and contrite heart.

Revelation 3:1–6,14–22
Psalm 15:2–3a,3bc–4ab,5
Luke 19:1–10

*He had the servants called, to whom he had given the money, to learn
what they had gained by trading. The first came forward and said, "Sir,
your gold coin has earned ten additional ones." He replied, "Well done,
good servant! You have been faithful in this very small matter; take
charge of ten cities."*
—LUKE 19:16–17

This parable tells the story of a nobleman who gave servants
gold coins and asked them to "engage in trade with these
until I return." One servant earned tenfold on his investment,
and the nobleman gave him more responsibility. However,
another servant did nothing. He put the coin in a
handkerchief because he was afraid. What has God entrusted
to me that I'm too afraid to use? My talents, gifts, resources?
Too many times I'm like the frightened servant—stuffing
everything God has given me into a handkerchief.

Revelation 4:1–11
Psalm 150:1b–2,3–4,5–6
Luke 19:11–28

NOVEMBER 22

• ST. CECILIA, VIRGIN AND MARTYR * THANKSGIVING DAY •

Sing to the LORD a new song
of praise in the assembly of the faithful.
—PSALM 149:1

For my daughter's hugs, a comfortable home, neighbors who stop by with warm soup, a husband who forgives me, conversation and wine with friends around the dinner table, the cardinal that visits the fruit trees in our backyard, a view of the sunrise from my writing desk, a new book project, health . . . for all these things I sing to the Lord a new song of praise. Sometimes I forget to give thanks. But today helps us remember.

Revelation 5:1–10
Psalm 149:1b–2,3–4,5–6a and 9b
Luke 19:41–44

• ST. CLEMENT I, POPE AND MARTYR * ST. COLUMBAN, ABBOT
* BLESSED MIGUEL AGUSTÍN PRO, PRIEST AND MARTYR •

> *In the way of your decrees I rejoice,*
> *as much as in all riches.*
> *Yes, your decrees are my delight;*
> *they are my counselors.*
> *The law of your mouth is to me more precious*
> *than thousands of gold and silver pieces.*
> *How sweet to my palate are your promises,*
> *sweeter than honey to my mouth.*
> —PSALM 119:14,24,72,103

Why do we resist following God's decrees and laws and
trusting in his promises? We think other things are the
answer—money, advice from others, satisfying our hunger in
whatever ways we can find. But as the psalmist writes, none
of those things can compare to the joy of following God.
How would our lives be different if we delighted in God's
promises and rejoiced in his decrees instead of yearning for
things that will never satisfy?

Revelation 10:8–11
Psalm 119:14,24,72,103,111,131
Luke 19:45–48

Saturday

NOVEMBER 24

• ST. ANDREW DŨNG-LẠC, PRIEST, AND COMPANIONS, MARTYRS •

"Teacher, you have answered well." And they no longer dared to ask him anything.
—LUKE 20:39–40

The Sadducees, who denied the Resurrection, posed a question to Jesus, hoping to trip him up and make a fool out of him. But of course, it didn't work. In response to their question about marriage after the Resurrection, Jesus patiently and eloquently answered them. His answer was brilliant enough to make them not dare ask another question. Likewise, our questions and complaining are no match for Jesus! Even so, he invites us to real conversation with him.

Revelation 11:4–12
Psalm 144:1b,2,9–10
Luke 20:27–40

NOVEMBER 25

• OUR LORD JESUS CHRIST, KING OF THE UNIVERSE •

"My kingdom does not belong to this world."
—JOHN 18:36

Pilate asks Jesus if he is king of the Jews. "My kingdom does not belong to this world," replies Jesus. The chief priests, Pilate, and angry crowds do not understand. They do not have the insight or imaginations to see beyond the literal or earthly definition of *kingdom*. Christ's dominion is not over earthly land or countries but over our hearts.

Daniel 7:13–14
Psalm 93:1,1–2,5 (1a)
Revelation 1:5–8
John 18:33b–37

*He said, "I tell you truly, this poor widow put in more than all the rest;
for those others have all made offerings from their surplus wealth, but she,
from her poverty, has offered her whole livelihood."*
—LUKE 21:3–4

When I sponsored a refugee family from Kosovo, my friends
and I spent weeks gathering clothes, bedding, furniture,
groceries, toys, and rent money to help them get settled. For
most of us, it wasn't a big sacrifice. We had extra clothes and
household items to spare. When we picked up the refugee
family from the airport, they carried one duffle bag that held
all their belongings. Yet the first thing they did was open
that bag and take out a box of candy to give to us. They had
so little, yet they gave what they had. How can we give out
of our own poverty?

Revelation 14:1–3,4b–5
Psalm 24:1bc–2,3–4ab,5–6
Luke 21:1–4

NOVEMBER 27

"All that you see here—the days will come when there will not be left a stone upon another stone that will not be thrown down."
—LUKE 21:6

I am writing this during an election year, and I am reminded how many people put all their hope in our democracy, our political parties, and whomever we elect president. And yet promises are made and broken, and every four or eight years it changes anyway. It seems that nothing gets done, each side refuses to compromise, and sometimes we think the system is broken. We have to remind ourselves that we can't put our hopes in this earthly kingdom. We need to put our hopes in the kingdom of God that shall never be destroyed.

Revelation 14:14–19
Psalm 96:10,11–12,13
Luke 21:5–11

NOVEMBER 28

Let the rivers clap their hands,
the mountains shout with them for joy.
Before the LORD, for he comes,
for he comes to rule the earth;
He will rule the world with justice,
and the peoples with equity.
—PSALM 98:8–9

"The arc of the moral universe is long, but it bends towards justice," said Martin Luther King Jr. Some days I wonder if this is true. Almost fifty years after King died, blacks and those who stand with them are still fighting for justice. When will it come, Lord Jesus?

Revelation 15:1–4
Psalm 98:1,2–3ab,7–8,9
Luke 21:12–19

NOVEMBER 29

Blessed are those who have been called to the wedding feast of the Lamb.
—REVELATION 19:9A

Our wedding took place on a warm day in May, when the trees and flowers were blooming and all our family members and friends were there. Most people would say that weddings are happy occasions, celebrating the union of two people. This story in Revelation paints a picture of the wedding feast of the Lamb, when the bridegroom (Christ) and the bride (the Church) are united. As Catholics, we get to participate in this wedding feast every Sunday at Mass. Throughout Church history, Catholic tradition has described Holy Communion—the culmination of the liturgy—as an intimate union with our divine Bridegroom, Jesus, in the Eucharist. So, go to Mass and enjoy your wedding feast!

Revelation 18:1–2,21–23; 19:1–3,9a
Psalm 100:1b–2,3,4,5
Luke 21:20–28

He called them, and immediately they left their boat and their father and
followed him.
—MATTHEW 4:21–22

It has always struck me how quickly the disciples decided to
follow Jesus. "Immediately they left their boat . . . and
followed him." What made them so confident and willing?
And how quickly would I have dropped my nets and left my
livelihood to follow Jesus?

Romans 10:9–18
Psalm 19:8,9,10,11
Matthew 4:18–22

DECEMBER 1

*Night will be no more, nor will they need light from lamp or sun, for the
Lord God shall give them light, and they shall reign forever and ever.*
—REVELATION 22:5

I am sitting in a hotel lobby in Iowa watching the sun come
up over the horizon, turning the sky from deep blue to pink
and orange. Yesterday, the weather was cold and blustery,
with freezing rain. What a relief to see the storm has passed,
and now the sky is clear again and the sun comes up over the
horizon. Today will be sunny—and sunny days in December
in the Midwest can be glorious—cold, clear, bright. How we
crave light. Now, as we enter the Advent season, we wait for
the Light of the World. Be hopeful even amid the storms,
because the sun is coming up soon.

Revelation 22:1–7
Psalm 95:1–2,3–5,6–7ab
Luke 21:34–36

DECEMBER 2

• FIRST SUNDAY OF ADVENT •

*The days are coming, says the LORD, when I will fulfill the promise I
made to the house of Israel and Judah.*
—JEREMIAH 33:14

One year, we had an unusually warm fall, and my friend Sue
told me that she even planted allium bulbs because the
ground was still soft and not yet frozen. These flowering
plants—part of the onion family—grow long stems and,
when they bloom, burst into a round flower that looks like a
purple ball, or fireworks. As we begin Advent, a season of
waiting, I think of these allium bulbs. For a long winter they
will remain below the ground, waiting for spring. But they
will not be still. The bulbs require a long period of cool
temperatures to spark the biochemical process that causes
them to flower. So it is with us. We wait for Christ. We wait
for the light. The days are coming, says the Lord, and our
souls are being prepared.

Jeremiah 33:14–16
Psalm 25:4–5,8–9,10,14
1 Thessalonians 3:12—4:2
Luke 21:25–28,34–36

DECEMBER 3

• ST. FRANCIS XAVIER, PRIEST •

"Lord, I am not worthy to have you enter under my roof; only say the word and my servant will be healed."
—MATTHEW 8:8

A few years ago, the language of the eucharistic liturgy was changed from "I am not worthy to receive you . . ." to "I am not worthy that you should enter under my roof, but only say the word and my soul shall be healed." At first I hated the change; it seemed awkward and strange. But then I learned the language comes directly from today's Scripture, when the Roman centurion asks Jesus to come into his home to heal his servant. The new language of the liturgy now seems more inclusive—not only do I want my own soul to be healed, but I want the healing of my soul to extend to my marriage, my family, my community. The more our souls are healed, the more capacity we have to love others into healing as well.

Isaiah 2:1–5
Psalm 122:1–2,3–4b,4cd–5,6–7,8–9
Matthew 8:5–11

DECEMBER 4

• ST. JOHN DAMASCENE, PRIEST AND DOCTOR OF THE CHURCH •

On that day . . .
The wolf shall be a guest of the lamb,
and the leopard shall lie down with the kid;
The calf and the young lion shall browse together,
with a little child to guide them.
—ISAIAH 11:1,6

"On that day," begins Isaiah 11:1. We wait with hope for that day, when the poor and those with dark skin will not have to deal with unjust systems, when black and white and brown will live together peacefully and equally, when we will all work together for the care of the environment, when politics will unify and heal, not divide and corrupt, when there will not be such huge income inequality, when hourly-wage workers will make enough money to feed their children, when talk show hosts will try to listen and understand the other side, not vilify them, when Facebook political discussions will be peaceful and loving, not hateful and angry. On that day.

Isaiah 11:1–10
Psalm 72:1–2,7–8,12–13,17
Luke 10:21–24

DECEMBER 5

> *On this mountain the LORD of hosts*
> *will provide for all peoples*
> *A feast of rich food and choice wines.*
> —ISAIAH 25:6

When my husband and I were looking for a house, we saw one we both liked immediately. It was a bungalow built in 1932 that had many original architectural details. The layout and updates were perfect for us. I had been praying for years that God would provide a house for us where we could build community, have more space for our daughter (and maybe other foster children), and have space for nieces and nephews to stay overnight. This house was it, and yet when we left the house, I said to David, "I think it's too nice for us," even though it was well within our price range. Do you, too, often have trouble noticing and accepting the abundance that God offers you? Today's Scripture reminds us that sometimes, God's gifts are extravagant.

Isaiah 25:6–10a
Psalm 23:1–3a,3b–4,5,6
Matthew 15:29–37

DECEMBER 6

• ST. NICHOLAS, BISHOP •

It is better to take refuge in the LORD
than to trust in princes.
—PSALM 118:9

During election years, it's easy to get caught up in politics.
We fight for our candidate and his or her positions. When
your candidate wins, it makes you feel like all will be right
with the world. But if your candidate loses, it can be
devastating and scary. As Christians, we cannot put our total
trust in politics or in presidents. We can fight to make things
better in this world and in our country, of course. But in the
end, only God, who sent his son to be born in a manger, can
sustain us and bring order and justice to the world.

Isaiah 26:1–6
Psalm 118:1 and 8–9,19–21,25–27a
Matthew 7:21,24–27

Friday

DECEMBER 7

• ST. AMBROSE, BISHOP AND DOCTOR OF THE CHURCH •

The LORD is my light and my salvation.
—PSALM 27:1

The days are getting shorter and shorter. The sunlight does not last long, especially if you live in the north. In Chicago, the sun hides behind clouds for much of winter. It's pitch dark when I leave work at 5:00 in the evening, and when I get home, I don't want to go out again—I just want to crawl under the covers and go to sleep. I struggle not to sink into a deep depression. I force myself to shop for Christmas gifts and get into the Christmas spirit. The writer Wendell Berry said, "It gets darker and darker and darker, and then Jesus is born." I wait in the dark with whatever hope I can muster.

Isaiah 29:17–24
Psalm 27:1,4,13–14
Matthew 9:27–31

DECEMBER 8

• THE IMMACULATE CONCEPTION OF THE BLESSED VIRGIN MARY
(PATRONAL FEASTDAY OF THE UNITED STATES OF AMERICA) •

"For nothing will be impossible for God."
—LUKE 1:37

Before I became a mother, when I longed for a child, my friend Kate gave me a cameo with an image of Mary on it. "Take this," she told me. "Maybe she will help you become a mother." I was skeptical, and yet, I kept the brooch in my jewelry box. I was in my forties, and I was giving up hope. When Mary asked the angel how in the world she could be pregnant when she was a virgin, the angel told her nothing was impossible for God. In fact, Mary's elderly, menopausal relative Elizabeth was also pregnant. How impossible was that? After a few miscarriages and seven years of trying to adopt, I got a call. It was about a little girl who needed a home. Like Mary, I said "Yes." Nothing is impossible for God.

Genesis 3:9–15,20
Psalm 98:1,2–3ab,3cd–4
Ephesians 1:3–6,11–12
Luke 1:26–38

DECEMBER 9

• SECOND SUNDAY OF ADVENT •

I am confident of this, that the one who began a good work in you will
continue to complete it
until the day of Christ Jesus.
—PHILIPPIANS 1:6

Some of us may get discouraged when we realize that we keep struggling with the same sins over and over. We may feel envious when a friend gets something we want, or resent all the work that parenting requires, or be too self-absorbed, lazy, or gluttonous. But this verse gives us hope, that one day we will be complete. That God is still working on us. The work of art he is creating is still in process.

Baruch 5:1–9
Psalm 126:1–2,2–3,4–5,6
Philippians 1:4–6,8–11
Luke 3:1–6

DECEMBER 10

"Which is easier, to say, 'Your sins are forgiven,' or to say,
'Rise and walk'?"
—LUKE 5:23

The paralyzed man's friends lowered him through the roof just so he could get a chance to be healed by Jesus. But before Jesus healed the man of his paralysis, he forgave his sins. Which is the bigger miracle? Jesus showed the crowd that the man had been healed ("Pick up your stretcher, and go home") and also that he had the authority to forgive sins. Forgiveness heals. When we know we are forgiven, we can let go of our shame and our unworthiness, pick up our mats, and go.

Isaiah 35:1–10
Psalm 85:9ab and 10,11–12,13–14
Luke 5:17–26

• ST. DAMASUS I, POPE •

Like a shepherd he feeds his flock;
in his arms he gathers the lambs,
Carrying them in his bosom,
and leading the ewes with care.
—ISAIAH 40:11

St. Damasus was pope from 366 to 384. He was a writer
though his talent was questionable. Some of his critics called
his work "lame and rigid." Ouch. But, like the descriptions of
God in today's Scripture, he was a true shepherd. St. Jerome
wrote, in a letter to Damasus: "Yet, though your greatness
terrifies me, your kindness attracts me. From the priest I
demand the safe-keeping of the victim, from the shepherd
the protection due to the sheep." How is God keeping you in
his care today?

Isaiah 40:1–11
Psalm 96:1–2,3 and 10ac,11–12,13
Matthew 18:12–14

And Mary said:
"My soul proclaims the greatness of the Lord;
my spirit rejoices in God my savior."
—LUKE 1:46–47

I can imagine the scene. Two pregnant women, both of whom had been visited by angels. One woman carrying the baby who will pave the way for the Lord and the other carrying Jesus. Can you picture the two of them, trading stories of the angels' announcements? Trying to comprehend the enormity of the situation? Maybe they had to convince each other that it was real. That they weren't just dreaming. But in this passage, it is obvious that they were incredulous and elated. When we know God is working in our lives—when he does great things—can we have any other response than to proclaim his greatness?

Zechariah 2:14–17 or
Revelation 11:19a; 12:1–6a,10ab
Judith 13:18bcde,19
Luke 1:26–38 or 1:39–47

DECEMBER 13

• ST. LUCY, VIRGIN AND MARTYR •

I will turn the desert into a marshland,
and the dry ground into springs of water.
—ISAIAH 41:18

One of my best friends lives in Arizona, and I love visiting her in the winter. The dry air, the sunshine, the desert foliage. I often visit a monastery while I'm there, and I sit near the labyrinth and watch the rabbits and desert birds among the scrub brush. But I'm always relieved to come home, where there are more trees and grass and water. I don't know if I could live somewhere that's so brown and dry. Water plays a big part in Scripture. Psalm 65:9 says, "You visit the earth and water it, you greatly enrich it," and in John 4:14, "but whoever drinks of the water that I will give him shall never thirst." Is your soul parched? If so, ask God to guide you to springs of his living water.

Isaiah 41:13–20
Psalm 145:1 and 9,10–11,12–13ab
Matthew 11:11–15

Blessed is the man who . . .
delights in the law of the LORD
and meditates on his law day and night.
—PSALM 1:1–2

Today we celebrate John of the Cross, a saint who grew up poor and was persecuted by his fellow monks, who jailed him in a six-by-nine-foot cell. During his life of suffering, he discovered that when he was stripped of everything, God was his only delight. He wrote that someone who seeks happiness in the world is like "a famished person who opens his mouth to satisfy himself with air." John wrote, "What more do you want, o soul! And what else do you search for outside, when within yourself you possess your riches, delights, satisfaction and kingdom—your beloved whom you desire and seek? Desire him there, adore him there. Do not go in pursuit of him outside yourself."

Isaiah 48:17–19
Psalm 1:1–2,3,4 and 6
Matthew 11:16–19

⇒ 377 ⇐

"But I tell you that Elijah has already come, and they did not recognize him but did to him whatever they pleased."
—MATTHEW 17:12

The Hebrew word for prophet is *nabi*, which means "to bubble forth, as from a fountain" or "to utter." Sometimes the Hebrew word *ro'eh*, which means "seer," is also used for prophets. In the Old Testament, the people were bitterly opposed to what the prophets were saying: that they should turn away from their golden idols because something much better was coming to redeem them. But they would not listen. They were afraid, stuck in their ways. How often do we ignore the words of God bubbling forth as if from a fountain?

Sirach 48:1–4,9–11
Psalm 80:2ac and 3b,15–16,18–19
Matthew 17:9a,10–13

DECEMBER 16

• THIRD SUNDAY OF ADVENT •

Then the peace of God that surpasses all understanding will guard your hearts and minds in Christ Jesus.

—PHILIPPIANS 4:7

During the Christmas season, we see and hear a lot about peace. Images of the Christ child in the manger and softly falling snow on Christmas Eve, candlelight services, choral concerts, the song "Silent Night"—all these things seem peaceful. But we may be anything but peaceful during this time. Maybe we are stressed about Christmas shopping, or too busy going to parties, or just plain lonely. When we are spiritually restored and in relationship with God, we will experience peace beyond all understanding. The Prince of Peace is here. He wants to give you his peace.

Zephaniah 3:14–18a
Isaiah 12:2–3,4,5–6 (6)
Philippians 4:4–7
Luke 3:10–18

Justice shall flower in his days,
and profound peace, till the moon be no more.
—PSALM 72:7

"Never forget that justice is what love looks like in public,"
says the philosopher and author Cornel West. One day,
justice shall flower—but until that time, we must keep on
loving. Cornel West also writes, "To be a Christian is to live
dangerously, honestly, freely—to step in the name of love as
if you may land on nothing, yet to keep on stepping because
the something that sustains you no empire can give you and
no empire can take away."

Genesis 49:2,8–10
Psalm 72:1–2,3–4ab,7–8,17
Matthew 1:1–17

DECEMBER 18

"Behold, the virgin shall be with child and bear a son,
and they shall name him Emmanuel."
—MATTHEW 1:23

Recently my daughter went through a time when she didn't
like being alone. I called her "my little barnacle" because she
wouldn't leave my side. Even now, she hates bedtime because
she doesn't want to be alone in her bedroom, even if I sit at
the kitchen table right outside her bedroom door where she
can see me. "Mommy, I just don't want to be alone!" she'll
wail. One time she said, "Mommy, what if you and Daddy
die? I will be all alone!" No, I tell her, "there are many people
who love you who would take care of you, and remember,
God is with you always."

Jeremiah 23:5–8
Psalm 72:1–2,12–13,18–19
Matthew 1:18–25

DECEMBER 19

After this time his wife Elizabeth conceived, and she went into seclusion for five months, saying, "So has the Lord done for me at a time when he has seen fit to take away my disgrace before others."
—LUKE 1:24–25

Elizabeth and Zechariah had been praying for a child for years. But maybe Elizabeth got to a point when she could no longer hope. Proverbs 13:12 says, "Hope deferred makes the heart sick." Maybe you know that sickness—that place where you are stuck in between hope and acceptance. Between desire and resignation. Between not knowing when or how to move on from a dream. The end of Proverbs 13:12 says, "But a longing fulfilled is a tree of life." A child satisfied a deep desire and longing in Elizabeth's life and gave her a great sigh of relief and joy, a validation of her purpose and calling. Be comforted by the fact that in that difficult space in between hope and resignation, God has not forgotten you.

Judges 13:2–7,24–25a
Psalm 71:3–4a,5–6ab,16–17
Luke 1:5–25

DECEMBER 20

Mary said, "Behold, I am the handmaid of the Lord.
May it be done to me according to your word."
—LUKE 1:38

I have a sticky note on my computer with a quote from the
comedian Tina Fey: "Say yes and you'll figure it out
afterwards." It reminds me to be open and willing to even the
things that are scary or feel like they are beyond me. Being
open and willing is an important posture to learn—it means
opening our hands to God and saying, "May it be done
according to your word." Mary said, Okay, God, I don't
totally understand this, and I'm afraid. But I trust you. She
said yes and gave birth to the Messiah. How many times
have you been reluctant to follow God? Just say yes and see
what great things God can do through you.

Isaiah 7:10–14
Psalm 24:1–2, 3–4ab, 5–6
Luke 1:26–38

My lover speaks; he says to me,
"Arise, my beloved, my dove, my beautiful one,
and come!"
—SONG OF SONGS 2:10

New love can be exhilarating—and if we are fortunate
enough to know that kind of love, we remember what it was
like to be overwhelmed by your partner, in a daze and willing
to do whatever he or she wanted. There are many ways to
think about Jesus—as a Judge, as a Savior, as a Shepherd,
and, in this passage, he is like a Lover. We are his beloved,
his beautiful one, his dove, and he is calling us to follow him.
How can we resist?

Song of Songs 2:8–14 or
Zephaniah 3:14–18a
Psalm 33:2–3,11–12,20–21
Luke 1:39–45

DECEMBER 22

"My soul proclaims the greatness of the Lord;
my spirit rejoices in God my savior.
for he has looked upon his lowly servant."
—LUKE 1:46–48

God used a lowly servant to bring salvation to the world.
Not a rich man, or a politician, or someone famous. A lowly
servant. Would any of those great men or women have said
yes to God? Or would they have been too busy and
self-important, well, selfish? Would they have had the
courage to surrender to God's will?

1 Samuel 1:24–28
1 Samuel 2:1,4–5,6–7,8abcd
Luke 1:46–56

DECEMBER 23

• FOURTH SUNDAY OF ADVENT •

Give us new life, and we will call upon your name.
—PSALM 80:19

In the beautiful children's book *Cry, Heart, But Never Break* by
Glenn Ringtved, Death comes into the house to explain to
the children why he has come to take their grandmother. He
tells the story of two brothers, Sorrow and Grief, who lived
their days "slowly and heavily" because "they never saw
through the shadows on the tops of the hills." Beyond those
shadows lived two sisters, Joy and Delight. One day, the two
brothers meet the two sisters and fall in love: Sorrow married
Joy, and Grief married Delight. Death says, "What would life
be worth if there were no death? Who would enjoy the sun if
it never rained? Who would yearn for the day if there were
no night?" If you're grieving this season, look beyond the
shadows to the tops of the hills.

Micah 5:1–4a
Psalm 80:2–3,15–16,18–19
Hebrews 10:5–10
Luke 1:39–45

DECEMBER 24

*In the tender compassion of our God
the dawn from on high shall break upon us,
to shine on those who dwell in darkness
and the shadow of death.*
—LUKE 1:78–79

On this Christmas Eve, I think of the shadow of death, which seems to be all around me these days. A friend was just diagnosed with breast cancer, another is dying of pancreatic cancer, civilians are dying in wars and terrorist attacks. We cannot escape the shadow of death. And yet, we wait in hope for our Savior. In his poem "Noel," J. R. R. Tolkien wrote: "The world was blind, the boughs were bent. / All ways and paths were wild: / Then the veil of cloud apart was rent, / And here was born a Child."

2 Samuel 7:1–5,8b–12,14a,16
Psalm 89:2–3,4–5,27 and 29
Luke 1:67–79

DECEMBER 25

• THE NATIVITY OF THE LORD (CHRISTMAS) •

So they went in haste and found Mary and Joseph, and the infant lying in the manger.
—LUKE 2:16

God presented himself to us in the most vulnerable way possible: a newborn lying in a manger. How delicately we hold a newborn baby. We cradle her head, carefully rock her in our arms, feel her soft, new skin. How can we do the same for ourselves and others this Christmas? "For those of us who celebrate Christmas," author Parker Palmer writes, "the best gift we can give others—whatever their faith or philosophy may be—is a simple question asked with heartfelt intent: What good words wait to be born in us, and how can we love one another in ways that midwife their incarnation?"

VIGIL:
Isaiah 62:1–5
Psalm 89:4–5,16–17,27,29
Acts 13:16–17,22–25
Matthew 1:1–25 or 1:18–25

DAWN:
Isaiah 62:11–12
Psalm 97:1,6,11–12
Titus 3:4–7
Luke 2:15–20

NIGHT:
Isaiah 9:1–6
Psalm 96:1–2,2–3,11–12,13
Titus 2:11–14
Luke 2:1–14

DAY:
Isaiah 52:7–10
Psalm 98:1,2–3,3–4,5–6
Hebrews 1:1–6
John 1:1–18

But they could not withstand the wisdom and the spirit with which he spoke.
—ACTS 6:10

St. Stephen was stoned to death because his message was too dangerous. The Sanhedrin didn't want to believe it. Author Richard Rohr says that most Christians believe the myth of redemptive violence—ignorant hating, excluding, and killing. In his book *Love Your Enemy: The Gospel Call to Nonviolence*, Rohr says Jesus replaces this with a new story of redemptive suffering. "The Gospel demands a great deal of us," he writes. "It calls us to a perennially unpopular and unselfish path. Little wonder Jesus said, 'The world's going to hate you.' When you can no longer play the game of judging, labeling, and punishing others, you will quickly become the outsider at most every cocktail party you attend. But Jesus has taught us how to hold the pain of the world until it transforms and resurrects us."

Acts 6:8–10; 7:54–59
Psalm 31:3cd–4,6 and 8ab,16bc and 17
Matthew 10:17–22

Thursday

DECEMBER 27

• ST. JOHN, APOSTLE AND EVANGELIST •

Then the other disciple also went in, the one who had arrived at the tomb first, and he saw and believed.
—JOHN 20:8

Some believed he was the Messiah when he was lying in the manger. Others believed when he healed the sick, or when he broke bread with them, or when he preached by the sea, or when he fed the 5,000. Others believed when they saw the empty tomb. God reaches into our lives at the exact moment when our hearts are thirsty and hungry and humble and open enough to say "Yes, I believe."

1 John 1:1–4
Psalm 97:1–2,5–6,11–12
John 20:1a and 2–8

⇒ 390 ⇐

*When Herod realized that he had been deceived by the magi, he became
furious. He ordered the massacre of all the boys in Bethlehem and its
vicinity two years old and under.*

—MATTHEW 2:16

We can embrace God's message of salvation or be threatened
by it. Herod, obviously, was threatened enough by Christ,
whom he feared would take away his power, that he ordered
him killed. And when he couldn't find the Christ child to kill,
he ordered that all the other male children in Bethlehem be
murdered. A horrible reaction, to be sure. The tiny,
vulnerable baby born in a manger certainly didn't enter the
world quietly. It was immediately apparent that something
big was happening—something that would change the
world—and us—forever.

1 John 1:5—2:2
Psalm 124:2–3,4–5,7b–8
Matthew 2:13–18

Saturday

DECEMBER 29

• ST. THOMAS BECKET, BISHOP AND MARTYR •

For the darkness is passing away, and the true light is already shining.
—1 JOHN 2:8

In Chicago it is dark and cold. The water in the birdbath out back has turned into one round block of ice. We have shoveled a path through the snow from the sidewalk to our front steps. My radiators hiss and bang, and the frost on the windows of our old bungalow creates abstract designs. Christmas Day has come and gone. We are waiting for the New Year. We have unwrapped gifts, visited family, celebrated with friends. But I am always a bit relieved when the holidays are over, because it will be a new year and the days will be longer, slowly but surely. Christ has come.

1 John 2:3–11
Psalm 96:1–2a,2b–3,5b–6
Luke 2:22–35

DECEMBER 30

• THE HOLY FAMILY OF JESUS, MARY, AND JOSEPH •

Beloved: See what love the Father has bestowed on us that we may be
called the children of God.

—1 JOHN 3:1

A few nights ago, Desta said, "Mommy, I'm so glad you and Daddy adopted me." My heart wanted to burst. Like many adopted children, Desta has at times been confused and ambivalent. She doesn't understand why we have different-colored skin, and she often asks about her birth mother. I look at her dark brown eyes. She can't understand now, but someday she will put the pieces of her story together, and I hope she will realize how beautiful it is and how beloved she is. As the adopted child of God, I too do not understand how my story will play out. But someday I will, and until then I will just be glad that he adopted me, and I will rest in his love.

1 Samuel 1:20–22,24–28 or
Sirach 3:2–6,12–14
Psalm 84:2–3,5–6,9–10 or
Psalm 128:1–2,3,4–5
1 John 3:1–2,21–24 or
Colossians 3:12–21 or 3:12–17
Luke 2:41–52